MARIA FRANKLAND

Write a Novel in a Year

Write a page every day: get support every step of the way

AUTONOMY
PRESS

First edition

This book was professionally typeset on Reedsy.
Find out more at reedsy.com

Write a Novel in a Year

Write a page every day: get support every step of the way

Contents

Join my ‘Keep in Touch’ list!

If you’d like to be kept in the loop about new books and special offers, join my ‘keep in touch’ list, and receive a free booklet, ‘The 7 S.E.C.R.E.T.S. to Achieving your Writing Dreams,’ visit www.mariafrankland.co.uk

This book is derived from a year-long online course which includes video, access to an online support group, further writing tasks and examples, links to further reading and the option of one-to-one support.

See https://mariafrankland.co.uk/how-to-write-a-novel/ for more information.

Introduction

There are many people who aspire to write a novel, and there is no doubt about what a tremendous accomplishment it is. However, many would-be novelists cite, 'I wouldn't know how to approach it,' or 'I never finish anything I start,' as reasons they never begin.

This book is derived from a class-taught and online course, which has been tried and tested by many writers, ensuring they go from the planning process through to the hugely enjoyable creation of scene after scene, then chapter after chapter, towards completion of that all-important first draft.

This book, as well as supporting the creation of your novel, will also develop your writing craft. In addition, it will give you the tools you will need to polish your first draft until it is good enough to be published. I write this both as a multi-published author, and as a creative writing teacher with an MA in Creative Writing.

There are publications that promise a completed novel in less time than a year, but speaking from experience, I know that a year is a realistic ambition.

I have divided the book into thirty sections with a view to around a fortnight being spent on each one. Of course, you can approach and complete each section as quickly or slowly as you need to, and you will probably find that you complete the earlier 'planning' sections much quicker than the later ones.

Underpinning this book is the requirement to write one A4 page every day (250 words.) Doing this for 365 days will ensure completion of a 90,000 word novel in a year.

You can complete your novel using this book as your guide, but there is also a companion workbook available to support the tasks and activities and give you space to reflect and to plan. Wherever you see [cwb] (companion workbook,) in the text, you will know there is a section in the accompanying workbook for you to write in.

Completion of your novel might be the dream, and I promise you that there is no feeling like holding your published book in your hands. At the time of writing, I am working on my seventh novel.

But the journey is just as enjoyable and rewarding as the destination. So enjoy every minute of it and I look forward to helping you all the way from planning to publication.

Preparing to Write a Novel

Welcome to the start of your exciting journey as a novelist! I can't wait to support you from beginning to end and to ensure that my guidance helps you achieve what is probably a long-held dream.

If you were taking this course in one of my face-to-face groups, or online, we would do one section every fortnight, but because this is a book, you can go as fast or as slow as you like, though I would impress on you, to take your time and revisit the exercises several times.

To thoroughly understand the material presented, spend at least two weeks on each chapter and come back periodically to a chapter, to refresh yourself.

I worked alone to write my first novel, which as a result, took me six years in total after a lot of false starts, life disasters and to-ing and fro-ing. I refined my process in subsequent novels, which enabled me to now show you the way to do it in one year. It is possible to work at one section per week and do double the daily prescribed word count – you will, of course, then finish in half a year!

This first section is dedicated to you beginning to plan the novel you want to write, and as a starting point, responding to the following questions [cwb1.1] will point you in the right direction:

1. Why do you want to write a book? *There could be several reasons. (money, ambition, freedom, etc.)*
2. What has stood in the way of you writing a book so far? *I will give lots of advice and support along the way, in terms of obstacles that get in the way for all writers.*
3. What place can you give yourself to write where you can create? *You might be lucky enough to have your own writing room or you may need to carve out a corner at home. Personally, my 'space' is a large pink stability ball in front of my coffee table!*
4. What improvements can you make to this space? *For example, a picture, a candle, lighting, music, etc.*
5. Is there a time of the day when you can usually devote half an hour to an hour for yourself? Mornings are good for me, when I'm fresh and full of creative energy. If I don't get my words out in the morning, it seems to 'hang over me' for the rest of the day.
6. When you miss any of these daily sessions, is there a good opportunity for you to catch up?
7. What unique experiences/events/settings have you lived through? *Drawing on what is familiar makes for an authentic and unique novel.* Although you are not writing a memoir here (I have another book and course for that!) but inevitably, your reality will creep into your fiction. I have a sign up in my office saying, *Careful, or you will end up in my novel!*

8. Finally, at this stage, have you any idea on what the novel might be that is trying to get out of you? *Don't worry if not, I offer support to help you generate your initial idea.*

To begin 'living as a writer,' I would like you to organise the following:

- Buy yourself a 'special' A4 notebook and pen which you will keep only for your writing – make it a hardback book with a design you love.
- Prepare your writing space – have a special cushion, picture, object, if need be.
- Carry a notebook and pen around with you – writers *notice* things. You never know when you will overhear a conversation or see something, perhaps in the landscape or a potential interesting 'character' that could spark a scene.

[cwb1.2] Make one observation each day as you go about your life. These should be things you see, hear, smell, taste or touch, as well as considering what feelings are evoked. Write a few lines about each observation. You need not do anything more with this (unless you want to!) At this stage, I want you to get into the habit of noticing things and capturing them in your notebook.

Generating your Idea

Writing is an activity that needs warming up towards, just like any other regular discipline. In my face-to-face classes, I always give a sentence starter or a theme to free-write with for five minutes. This act of warming up helps you make the transition from your bustling everyday self into your writing self.

[cwb2.1] Here are a few ideas for you to fall back on for future writing warm-ups:

- Sentence Starter: The day started like any other.
- Write an argument or reconciliation between two characters.
- Write about a beginning, or an ending.
- Write about two characters parting, or reuniting.
- Your favourite place
- The seaside…
- A perfect day…
- 'Is this seat taken,' said a voice she was sure she recognised…

To exercise your 'writing muscle,' today, I would like you to respond to the following writing prompts:

- *The day after my tenth birthday, my mother told me ...* (write five sentences.) [cwb2.2]
- *Describe an accident ...* (write five sentences.) [cwb2.3]
- *Describe a situation in which two people disagree.* [cwb2.4]
- *Imagine you're alone looking through the window from the outside? What can you see and how does it make you feel?* [cwb2.5]

Genre

From your thoughts and answers so far, what sort of novel genre do you feel most drawn towards? Do your responses fit into one or more of the genres below? It can be equally valuable to identify which genres you want to rule out. Personally, I find that no matter what I try to write, it ends up as a psychological thriller! And I wouldn't dream of tackling several of the genres on the list below! Perhaps you will be the same.

- Crime/thriller
- Mystery
- Western
- Fantasy
- Supernatural
- War
- Romance
- Issue
- Family Drama/Saga
- Autobiographical
- Comedy
- 'Adult'
- Children's

- Horror
- Biographical
- Teenage
- Science Fiction
- Historical

Of course, you can choose more than one genre in respect of what you might like to write, and there is usually some overlap, anyway. Often what you like to write is what you enjoy reading, and as I will keep mentioning, it's so important to read as much as possible when you're a writer.

Don't put too much pressure on yourself to make a firm genre decision - it's still early days, and you might change your mind as we move through the planning phase.

Research

[cwb2.6] If you already have an idea for the novel you want to write, give some thought and make a list with respect to the research that might be necessary, prior to writing it. How and where can you carry this research out?

We are so lucky nowadays to have the internet at our disposal though, as a crime writer, I sometimes worry what might be made of my internet search history if it was to ever to be examined!

[cwb2.7] Whilst deciding how much research you might be willing and able to do, consider the following questions:

- Why is research important?
- What happens if it is not carried out effectively?
- At what stage in a novel, should it be carried out?

Writers Notice Things

Earlier, I suggested carrying a notebook around, to get you accustomed to recording your observations as you go about your daily life. Writers are nosy – we notice things! [cwb2.8] Throughout the next week, respond to the observation prompts below. (Without getting arrested!) Perhaps one each day.

One or more of them might generate an idea for a story or scene within a story as you continue gathering ideas through this planning phase of the course.

1. Notice an interesting person – who might they be? What might their background story be?
2. Note down the key points of an interesting conversation you overhear?
3. What do you notice around you whilst waiting in a queue?
4. Observe a couple you don't really know – what might their problems be?
5. Observe something that's natural and scenic within your neighbourhood.
6. Choose a neighbour you don't know. Imagine what is their greatest (1) regret and (2) achievement.

Enjoy this time of nosiness! It is a pre-requisite for every writer!

Character Creation

Once you have decided on the genre you will write in, character development is a great place to go next.

Hopefully, you are enjoying the process of 'being nosy' and making observations in your notebook, which will be useful for the novel you are about to write. Being aware of the people who surround you can be wonderful for the creation of character as well.

You may already have a main character in mind for your novel or you may find a picture of a 'character' on-line or in a magazine (not a celebrity.) Google images is a good place to look.

[cwb3.1] Alternatively, write out a physical sketch of a character you have in mind. This is how I usually work and I often base my characters on someone I have met fleetingly or take slivers of the truth from people I know! (I have already mentioned the *'Careful, or you will end up in my novel'* sign which I have in my house!) Most people know to be wary of a novelist!

So, whether you are using a picture, your memory, or your

imagination to bring a visual representation of your character, you are now going to get to know your main character in more depth. Often the rest of the story will start to emerge from this process.

Getting to Know your Character

[cwb3.2] It is important that you know your main character *inside and out* before you bring them to the page. You should be able to visualise them, hear them speak and know what makes them tick. If you do not know them well, it is difficult for your readers to get to know them too.

The following prompts will help you become familiar with your character, even if lots of these details do not actually make it into your novel. This familiarity will ensure that your character starts to live and breathe within you – it's a really exciting process, so allow them your headspace, and continue to get to know them, even beyond this activity.

- Full name:
- Age:
- Home and Family Information:
- Medical Conditions:
- Bad Habit:
- Sleeping Patterns:
- Favourite Clothes:
- Driving Habits:
- Occupation:
- Hobbies and Interests:
- Two things they did yesterday:

- One thing they must do tomorrow:
- A talent they have been told they possess:
- Something they are embarrassed about:
- Something they would like to do before they die:
- The most special thing they own:
- Something or someone that makes them laugh:
- The hardest thing they have ever had to do:
- Their happiest memory:
- Their favourite place:
- Something they once did that was helpful:

Internal Monologue

[cwb3.3] Next, have your character introducing their self. Start with *hello, my name is ...* then write a few sentences saying who they are.

Then, when you read this monologue aloud, the way you speak will help you become better acquainted with your character and you will be able to 'hear' their voice along with any accent and socio-economic status you are giving them. This might sound like a strange thing to do, but I promise it works!

Next, put your character into a *situation*

Now you have started to get to know your character, you will become even better acquainted when you consider their reactions when placed in a variety of situations and challenges.

[cwb3.4] Choose one or more scenarios best suited to your character and build it into a scene. The more you choose, the more familiar you will become with your character's personality, voice and mannerisms.

I recommend not to 'overthink' the prompts but write whatever comes to you first. And please, whatever you do, don't worry about making anything perfect at this stage, just free write. I'm giving you carte blanche not to be concerned with spelling, grammar, punctuation or layout! That all comes later. Give your scenes a beginning, middle and conclusion.

- Your character is reunited with someone they have not seen for a long time.
- Your character asks someone else a peculiar question.
- Whilst out for a walk with a loved one, your character notices the mushroom cloud of a nuclear bomb.
- Someone your character knows well pulls out a gun and shouts, 'one of us is going to die!'
- Your character decides they can make a living out of selling a particular thing.
- Your character finds a diamond bracelet in the street.
- Your character's brother wins the lottery.
- Your character is asked for a loan of £5000.
- Your character notices people laughing at them whilst they're in a shopping centre.
- Your character discovers their sister is a liar and a cheat.
- Your character meets someone famous.
- Your character returns home to find they have been burgled.
- Your character knows what they are about to do is forbidden.

Now that you have had fun putting your character into a host of volatile situations, it is time to decide on the setting you will use for the opening of your novel...

Story Settings

There is more than first meets the eye to consider when bringing a setting to life in a story. Personally, I draw on the familiar, so I wouldn't try to set my story somewhere that I hadn't visited or at least done some hefty research around. What is even more powerful is if you can actually sit and write in the setting you are using for your story.

So yes writers, you have my full permission to book yourself a flight to the Canaries if that's where you're planning to set your novel!

Why is 'place' important in a novel?

- Human relationships don't occur in a vacuum – they must take place in an *environment.*
- Settings can tell us about the era in which the story is taking place. For example, if I was to include a 'twin tub' in a story, you could safely assume the era was the seventies or eighties. I'm showing my age now!
- Settings can tell us about other issues prevalent in the story. For example, strewn ashtrays, unwashed cups and piles of unopened bills might say something about a character's

socio-economic status.

- Good setting descriptions can pull the reader into the story and really show what is going on. As writers, our job is to help our readers *visualise.*
- Place tells the reader something about the character from their relationship with the setting and their feelings about it. For example, a character entering a situation with trepidation and unease may associate the place with a bad memory.
- Certain settings are synonymous with the story genre, for example, my domestic thrillers contain the home, courts rooms, police stations, prisons, funeral parlours, and crematoriums.

What should we be aiming for when bringing a setting to life?

- A *cinematic approach.* Imagine the scene being 'staged.' And what writer doesn't dream of having their book made into a film or TV screenplay?
- A 'drip feed' of setting details through the narrative, rather than giving information in one dense paragraph.
- All five senses should be used but smell is particularly evocative. A good setting description can automatically transport a reader into the world you are creating.
- Atmosphere – darkness, temperature and a character's physical reaction to a place can further bring a setting to life. In opposition to this, so can sunshine, music and pleasant conversation.

[cwb4.1] **Considering how setting is used**

A good starting point is to consider the use of setting in already-published novels. I suggest that you take a section which concentrates on setting and consider the following questions:

1. What relationship, if any, exists between character and place?
2. What has the writer focused on? Why do you think this is?
3. How are sensory and physical impressions evoked?
4. How are mood and emotion created?

There are no right or wrong answers; this is just an opportunity for you to consider the use of setting further.

[cwb4.2] **Create the initial setting for your own novel**

Look for a picture of an interior or exterior setting which could be used for the opening scene of your novel.

Whether you are working from a picture or an image in your mind, jot down a description of your setting. Use lots of sensory information, (sight, sound, smell, touch and taste.) Or as mentioned before, if you can physically be immersed in the setting, that is even better!

[cwb4.3] **Put your character into their setting**

Next, you will put the character you have already invented into your setting, and write a scene that may be suitable for inclusion in your novel.

1. Have your character enter the setting. Use a verb to portray the mood they are in, (e.g. stamped.)
2. Have them look at something which triggers a memory, (this could be recent or distant.)
3. Have your character performing an action of some sort – *doing* something.
4. Have one of your secondary characters enter the setting and a dialogue take place between the two characters. This is an excellent opportunity to get to know one of your secondary characters better. (You will be getting to know your secondary characters in much more depth soon.)

Have your main character leave the setting, thinking something to themselves as they leave.

Your Overall Plan

Are you a 'plotter or a pantser?'

Some authors launch straight into their novel (pantsers!) I love this term – basically it means flying on the seat of your pants and lots of authors swear by this *discovery writing*. But arguably, perhaps if there is an idea of destination *before* departure, there is a better chance of arrival! (plotter.)

I am a bit of a cross between plotter and pantser. I make sure I know my main characters and initial setting before I set off and I also have a brief outline of the story plotted out. I then bullet point the chapters, two or three in advance. Having a skeleton outline of your novel ensures less likelihood of stalling along the way, as you always have a plan to refer to.

This 'plan' is not 'set in stone' and you may deviate from it. I use mine as a 'working document' and annotate it as the novel progresses. Our characters can often surprise us, and a story can suddenly take off in a different direction. This is one of the most exciting aspects of being a writer, when they take on a life of their own.

[cwb5.1] **Where, When, Who, What and Why**

The following prompts should offer some starting points for your novel:

Where is the main action? **(Setting)** *Refer back to the section on setting. You could also list other settings that may occur in your novel.*

When does it happen? **(Timespan and era)** *What duration will your story cover? In what era? If a short duration, what time of year?*

Who is involved? **(Main characters)** *Your central character (protagonist) has been worked on. Soon, you will be getting to know your secondary characters in more depth too. If you already know who some of them might be, make a note of them now.*

What will happen? **(brief plot outline)** *This is the trickier part! Can you give a brief outline of your* ***plot*** *in just a few sentences? Consider the beginning, middle and end of your novel, and think about what it is your character is trying to achieve and what is standing in their way. It is this 'obstacle' aspect that creates the conflict necessary for story.* Even if you just have the bones of something at the moment, write it down – you can keep adding to it as you go along.

Why will people want to read your story? (What is its '**Unique Selling Point**?') *What is going to be different about your book? Why are you writing it? What is special about it? You must keep this in mind at all stages – it will keep you moving forwards.*

[cwb5.2] **The overview of your novel**

You could use a 'bullet point' approach to outline your story's possible progression

- Opening Scene:
- next
- then, etc
- _
- _
- _
- _
- _
- Climax:
- Resolution.

Stories are often 'arc-shaped' and consist of the beginning, then rising action, which ebbs and flows to a point of climax, which then simmers down to the story resolution.

This same 'arc' applies to the individual chapters that build to construct a novel; that is each chapter should offer a 'rising tension' and end on a 'mini-cliffhanger' to encourage a reader to keep reading.

To a lesser extent, the individual scenes contained within chapters should reflect this 'story arc;' each scene with its own beginning, middle and end and consisting of the rising action and 'mini cliffhanger.'

We will deal with the construction of chapters and scenes later in the book.

The Opening and Second Paragraph

Grab your reader by the throat, is something I once heard at a writing workshop. As a crime writer, I liked this line and I've never forgotten it! Many readers won't read past the first couple of pages if you *don't* grab them.

An engaging story opening needs to contain an element of surprise for the reader, whilst hooking them into your character and setting, right from the beginning. Part of this is making them *care* about your character and their situation as quickly as possible. It is this emotional connection that will ensure they read on.

Try to embody as many of the following into your opening paragraphs:

- **A character:** The reader wants to meet someone straight away. They hope to feel some emotional connection or empathy with your character.
- **The setting or subject matter:** The reader needs to orientate themselves. They will know where they are and/or what's going on. They want to read about somewhere or something they find intriguing and interesting.

- **Motivation:** The reader wants to know something about the personality of the character(s) they're meeting. Are they nervous? Extrovert? Obsessive?
- **Action:** Something must be happening, or just about to happen; They want the story to begin and not be offered too much backstory. Perhaps you can enter your novel at a point of dialogue. This will pull a reader straight in.
- **Sensual detail:** The reader wants to be transported into the world of the book; for this to happen their senses need to be engaged with concrete, vivid detail. All the senses need to be considered, not just the visual.
- **A limit on description:** What the reader doesn't want is lots of description – start at a point of action and allow any description to be 'drip-fed' throughout the narrative. I have been guilty of beginning novels with a load of 'backstory' to explain to the reader what has gone before. It then becomes necessary to hit the delete key on the first two or three paragraphs, (always painful!) Backstory is best 'drip-fed' through the narrative.

To prepare for writing your own novel, it will be helpful for you to consider some openings of novels you have read.

You can then compare the elements listed above with your chosen openings.

For example, *do we meet a character straightaway? Are we immediately taken into the setting? What has the writer done to make sure that you 'care' enough to keep reading?*

Some Ways of Beginning a Story

Adapt one of these as a starting point if you haven't already got a first line in mind.

1. <insert name> is able to do something I've always envied – to stop any man in the street.
2. "Is this seat taken?" said a voice <insert name> was sure he recognised.
3. He had always been a leader …
4. I decided to ignore …
5. She had always dreamed of …
6. I had forgotten …
7. She grappled around the room for her phone before pummelling at the buttons.

Now you can bring your character and setting to the page

[cwb6.1] Write your opening paragraph. Try to begin at a point of action. Lots of novelists make the mistake of starting too soon and giving too much backstory, which is necessary but should be 'drip-fed' throughout the novel, like me!

[cwb6.2] Once you have written your opening paragraph, write your second one, keeping in mind the elements above. Then continue writing until you have filled your first page with 250 words.

Remember what I said in the introduction. A mere 250 words every day becomes 7500 in a month, which leads to a lovely novel sized 90,000 words over a year. You can do it!

It is now time to continue writing a 250 word page every day. There will be times, of course, when life gets in the way, but if you can get into a momentum and routine, you will have your first draft completed within the intended timescale.

There will be days when you cannot bear to stop after a page or two, and need to keep writing. This will compensate for days when you cannot find the time.

Consider leaving your work mid-sentence as it becomes easier to pick it back up the next day. I pinched this idea from Ernest Hemingway and can tell you it works.

The act of creation is the most enjoyable part of writing your novel. Don't just focus on the end result – enjoy the journey!

The one rule is *create only*; do not try to edit anything until after you have got completely to the end of your novel's first draft. Having said that, I do advise just *reading* back over what you have written the previous day to orientate yourself back into the story.

This exciting first draft is just *you*, telling the story to *yourself*. It is the best part of the process where you have free rein to be imaginative, creative and just let that story emerge.

I am even saying that you don't have to worry about spelling, punctuation, or grammar. Not yet! There is a section on editing later in the book.

Secondary Characters

Whilst you are writing your now unfolding novel, it is important to give your secondary characters their own 'sub plots' and motivations. This helps to ensure your novel is well-rounded and realistic.

A large part of what will build pace and suspense is the interaction between all your characters. The *emotion* between them all is what will keep your reader hooked. In this section, you will get to know your secondary characters almost as well as your main character. I love this process – before long, you will find that your characters almost inhabit you and you literally hear their voices when you are thinking about your story. I promise you're not going mad!

Who are your Secondary Characters?

Your secondary characters are the characters whereby your novel would 'fall down' without them. (Not your 'bit-part' characters who may only come in for a scene or two.) A good starting point is the construction of a 'spidergram' which will show the relationships and hierarchy of your characters.

Place your central character in a circle at the centre of your page and the secondary characters around it, in circles at the end of 'spider legs,' writing along these 'legs' what each relationship is to the central character.

You could then draw lines between the secondary characters, showing what their relationships are to one another. You can add as much information as you need to.

[cwb7.1] **Complete the following for EACH significant character in your novel**

- Name:
- Age:
- Appearance and dress:
- Relationship to Main Character:
- Involvement in Main Character's Story:
- Feelings towards Main Character: *(this is the interesting bit!)*
- What is their goal and motivation? *(sub-plot)*
- What is standing in their way?
- Back Story:

Introductory Monologue which relates to main character: *Have them introducing themselves but within that, making reference to the main character - read this aloud – you will get a sense of their accent, way of speaking and overall voice.*

You may feel silly to begin with but this is a really powerful process of getting to know your character.

A page a day: You should now be writing one handwritten A4 pages every day (250 words.) As I have previously mentioned, don't try to edit, just keep moving forwards.

Remember to keep enjoying the creative process - *don't worry about making things 'perfect' just yet – there will be plenty of time to edit your novel later.*

Dialogue

We writers are a diverse bunch. Some of us predominantly deliver our novels through 'action.' Some through the 'internal' thoughts of the main character. Others rely mostly on description and exposition.

Personally, I am a dialogue driven writer and prefer this sort of novel as a reader too. I want to hear what the characters are saying to one another and how they are saying it. The style which you enjoy reading, may also be how you enjoy writing.

This section will concentrate on dialogue, but as you progress through the course, I will deal with the other elements of driving narrative too.

Dialogue has many functions:

- It reveals characters' relationships to each other. Relationships can be 'shown' rather than 'told,' by what the characters say to one another and how they interact.
- It offers information about a character and give details about where they live, their background and social standing, and shows what sort of person they are.

- It can move the story forwards. Dialogue really brings the narrative to life. It enables the reader to visualise what is taking place and to hear the voices of the characters.
- Dialogue breaks up blocks of narration. Many readers, me included, are 'put off' when presented with a dense page of text. Our eyes naturally run over a piece of text, punctuated with dialogue, much more easily.
- Spoken interaction between characters increases the tension. Drama is created by *what* is said and *how* it is said, although equally, what we do not say can also add to the tension.
- Sometimes a character's 'internal thought' can be placed alongside dialogue. Only that of your viewpoint character, though! We will return to internal thought in a later section.

'Rules' when writing dialogue (You may want to compare the below guidance to already published books to get a feel for the finished layout and appearance.)

- Speech marks go on the outside of punctuation marks.
- Try not to overuse speech tags, (replied, asked, said, etc,) and when you do use them, keep them simple; there is no need for murmured, screamed, extrapolated! – too much could jar the reader out of your story.
- New speaker - new line.
- Use character action to break up the dialogue. *This is important. You can show anger, excitement, etc by what a character does and how they do it. (e.g. Sarah slammed the book onto the table. "I can't do it!")* Using this method also

shows the reader who is speaking without having to rely on speech tags.

- Go easy on the adverbs (happily, slowly, etc.) Rather than using an adverb, show *how* something is being said through the spoken words and the way the character is acting.
- Read your dialogue aloud to check it flows. (At editing stage – don't worry about this yet!)
- Keep it interesting. Avoid any mundane conversation that doesn't move your story along. Unless it's relevant, your readers probably don't need to hear a conversation about the weather or the price of potatoes!

What you like/dislike about the following two short examples of dialogue? Which extract would you be most likely to continue reading?

"You lied to me," said Sarah.

"We did it to protect you." Joe placed his cup back on its saucer.

Roger stepped towards Sarah and reached for her hand. "We didn't want you to get hurt—"

Sarah pushed his hand away and turned from them. "I thought I could trust you both. How could you do this to me?"

***

"I saw Joe in the park the other day," said Neil.

"Oh did you," said Janet. "How is he doing?"

"He has a new job. He has flexible working hours, so he has lots more free time," said Neil.

"Well good for him," said Janet. "Do you know what he wants to do with his free time?"

"No, I meant to ask him that," said Neil.

"Why didn't you?" asked Janet.
"I forgot, to be honest," replied Neil.

[cwb8.1] **Choose one of the scenarios below to practise writing dialogue.**

Pay attention to setting it out. At this stage, keep the dialogue between just two characters.

- A man suggests to his girlfriend she gets cosmetic surgery.
- Two strangers are sharing a seat on a long bus journey. One of them needs a place to stay.
- A wife kidnaps a baby. Her husband finds her changing nappies and wants to know what is going on.
- Two people are on a date. One of them is far more interested than the other.
- A teenager redecorates his parent's home whilst they are away. They arrive back home unexpectedly early.
- A young woman wants her flatmate to move out.

[cwb8.2] **Next, Write a Scene for your Novel**

As you approach the next scene in your novel, make sure it is driven by dialogue. As you continue to work on your novel, use dialogue wherever you can to drive your story forward. Never *tell* a reader about a conversation, e.g. x and y had an argument, rather, play the argument out and *show* it to your reader.

I find, as a writer, that my characters literally 'take off' when they are talking to one another. To lead this interaction between them is really exciting.

Show, Don't Tell

The golden rule that needs to be adhered to by all writers is, *show, don't tell.* This allows the reader to experience a story for themselves through action, words, thoughts, senses and feelings rather than through summary and description. It enables the reader to be 'in the moment' and to have the opportunity to interpret details in the text, making reading a more active process.

My first drafts are often very 'telling,' until, usually, third draft stage, then I will ensure I'm 'showing' more, and enabling the reader to do some work.

Where an author does 'show, don't tell' *well,* the reader can be really 'in the moment,' feeling and experiencing events alongside the characters. Using narrative elements such as character action, sensory language, dialogue, description and internal thought can reduce telling within story, and make it more showing. Brief examples of how to *show* are below.

Using Character Action: *Continuing along the lane, her pace quickened with each step. She kept looking behind, hearing her heartbeat thudding in her ears.* <u>Here, the emotion of fear is</u>

conveyed through the character's walk. It is not necessary to say 'she was scared.'

Using Sensory Language: *The smell took her right back. It was the aftershave he'd worn when they'd been dating.* In this instance, smell conveys nostalgia. 'She missed him' is not needed.

Using Dialogue: *"Thomas Clifford," Mum stood at the door with her hands on her hips. "Get in here this instant!"* The reader can infer that Mum is angry.

Using Description: *He cradled the guitar in his arms like a lover. Together, they had created history.* That the character loves his guitar and is proud of something, is obvious.

Using Internal Thought: "It's fine, honestly." Dan folded his arms. *You'll get what's coming to you...* Dan is planning something, and things are not fine. We are shown this, rather than told.

[cwb9.1] **Complete the following exercises, aiming to write scenes to be included in your novel. It is possible to use more than one of them within the same scene.**

Character Action: Have your main character taking a walk and showing through how s/he is walking (e.g. creeping,) how they are feeling.

Sensory Language: Have your main character hearing, seeing, smelling, tasting or touching something which makes them recall a memory. What effect does it have on them?

Dialogue: Engage one character in a conversation with another character. Show their mood through what is being said.

Description: Use a possession, belonging to your one of your characters, to portray something of your character's personality – show how s/he feels about it.

Internal Thought: Through your character's thinking, give details of something they are planning and their emotion about it.

'Show, don't tell,' is a writing skill that develops over time, and is something that really needs to be worked on at in the beginning. So don't worry if you find it difficult. When we get into the editing process, I will talk you through a 'checklist' of things to look for.

Narrative Voice

Narrative 'voice' is the telling of a story which affects the style, tone and attitude in which the story is being told. It is linked to *'viewpoint'* which we will explore later. I have purposely separated these two elements of writing, to avoid confusion.

An early decision we need to make as writers is *whose story is it?* And *which character do I want the reader to connect with?* Remember, the greatest connections are achieved emotionally.

'Voice' comes from *what* and *how* a character sees the fictional world they are inhabiting and what they think about it.

The language they choose to express themselves is also important–their words, phrases, accent and slang need to be chosen carefully, in order that they remain true to that character.

The better a writer knows their character before they bring them to the page, the more distinct their voice is, not only from the other characters but from the author's own voice.

I ultimately have my novels recorded as audio books, so I've constantly got that distinction of voice in my mind. Perhaps it will also help you to keep in mind how your characters will sound in audio. (*And this is something you should consider—audio books are big news right now!*)

Use a personal anecdote to experiment with voice

[cwb10.1] Write a memorable autobiographical event in your own voice, using the pronoun I/me/my. It can be happy, sad or funny.

Ensure it involves a second character. *If you are struggling to think of an event, try one of the following:*

- Wedding
- Christmas
- Milestone Birthday
- Interview
- Medical Appointment

[cwb10.2] Write an account of the same event, but this time, in the voice of a second character, (still using the pronoun I/me/my,) and ensuring the voice is distinct from yours. Note how it changes.

[cwb10.3] **Return now to your novel and ask yourself:**

Have I chosen the right character to take the story forward? *You could try writing an already-written scene in the voice of another character to consider this.*

What emotional aspects have I used which enable the reader

to connect to/with the main character? What will make them care?

Is their voice distinct from other characters in the story?

Is the way they speak and think relatable?

Is their voice consistent throughout the story?

Tense

The tense you write in can have a huge effect on your story. It is worth experimenting to see whether swapping tense can improve your story before you go any further with your novel.

The most common tense used is past, however present tense is being used more now. An explanation and examples, of past and present tense, are given below.

Past

As noted, to tell a story in past tense is more usual than using other tenses, relating back to the days of verbal storytelling and relating tales. Any story can be given further authenticity if told as though it has already happened.

<u>Example</u>

"No, I won't. I don't look at your phone." He reached for the kitchen door handle. "If you don't trust me, it's your problem." She lunged at the pocket he was guarding with his other hand. "Get off me!" She grasped his arm. Her nails bore into it. "You're hurting me!"

Present

Telling stories in present tense is becoming more popular, especially in genres like crime and thrillers. It gives a sense of immediacy and increases the closeness between the reader and the story, in that they feel as though they are experiencing the action as it is unfolding.

Example

Paul sits, staring into space, whilst he reluctantly spoons cereal into his mouth. His insides churn with every spoonful, yet he knows he needs every ounce of energy to get through the day before him. This is the big one. It is possible that by the end of this day, he might know his fate.

[cwb11.1] Re-write a scene from your novel you have already written, considering the effect when you change the tense of the story.

For example, if you have written in past tense, try changing it into present. ('I turned from him and walked away' becomes 'I turn from him and walk away.') Or vice versa. ('she looks at me in a way that makes me uncomfortable,' becomes 'she looked at me in a way which made me uncomfortable.')

Now is the time to change things before you go much further if you prefer the 'changed' version.

Building Scenes

We can think of a novel as a series of 'building blocks,' as touched on in the 'planning' section. The novel is the 'whole' and follows a story 'arc.'

A typical 'story arc' is the beginning and **introduction** of a story with its characters, situation and setting, followed by the **rising action** with all its ups and downs, building towards the **climax** then finally the **resolution**.

When I'm talking about this concept in the classroom, usually, the group of writers I'm working with are laughing at me waving my arms around, frantically trying to demonstrate this 'building blocks' approach.

Holding the novel together as a 'whole,' are the chapters which build progressively on top of each other.

Each chapter should also follow that 'arc' with a beginning, a middle and an end, but leave on a 'cliffhanger' so the reader will want to read on. This 'arc' is on a less dramatic scale to the 'whole novel' arc.

Then, each chapter should comprise four to seven scenes which should also follow the story 'arc,' but to a lesser extent still, this concept will be returned to in the next section - building chapters. I hope that makes sense – maybe the 'waving around of the arms approach' is more beneficial!

As mentioned before, I'm a *bit* of a planner so must again advocate this approach to you. Already, you have done some planning around your novel. Now that you're getting going, you will probably find it helpful to have some further planning tools at your disposal. Here's some planning advice you can try prior to writing new scenes.

[cwb12.1] **Before writing a scene (or even whilst editing one you've already written,) consider the following:**

What needs to happen in this scene? The key word here is 'needs' - you must keep the story moving forward using conflict, intrigue and action, so come up with a sentence or two that explains what absolutely must happen next in your story.

What would happen if I omitted this scene? If your computer accidently deleted this scene, would the novel still make sense? If the answer is yes, that you don't need the scene and should probably move forwards without it. This is tremendously difficult to discern!

Who needs to be in the scene? Novels are sometimes clogged with unnecessary characters who make the odd appearance and then do not say or do anything else for pages and pages. Make sure your characters all have a role and that they drive your story forwards. Two or three 'bit part' characters can be amalgamated into one character. I do this a lot.

Where could the scene take place? Often the most obvious place for a scene is the least interesting, so don't be too quick to set your scene in the car or the living room.

What's the most surprising thing that could happen in this scene? Step away from your outline and consider some wild possibilities. We can also do this to 'liven things up' at editing stage. What if a bus smashed through the wall? What if one of your characters suddenly choked and died? Most of your scenes won't have 'out of nowhere' aspects, but a novel should have a few moments that are unexpected – could this scene contain one of them?

Is this a long or a short scene? Ask yourself, how much screen time am I willing to give to this scene? You can easily spend three pages on a scene before realising as much could have been accomplished in a single page. This again, is something you may make a decision on at editing stage.

Brainstorm three different ways the scene could begin Of course, you need to be clear on how your previous scene has just ended. Then, come into your new scene as late as you possibly can, at a point of action, rather than opening with a preamble.

Use an image or line of dialogue to open with but don't stop at your first option. Always consider what the characters will be doing and thinking alongside the dialogue you are writing for them. There will be more about this 'interweaving' elements of story soon.

Planning your Scene

Below are some different strategies for planning a scene before you write it:

Play it on a screen in your head [cwb12.2] A part of novel writing can be sitting with closed eyes, allowing yourself some space and time to watch the unwritten scene within your mind.

It will start off vague, but eventually you should hear the characters talking to each other. Don't worry if you can't get the scene to play right through – you will find the ending to it more in the writing than in the imagining.

Write a Scribble Version [cwb12.3] This reminds you of the scene you have just imagined. Don't write sentences, just a series of bullet points to ensure you won't forget what you want to include. Your scribble version probably would not make sense to anyone but you, and exists only to ensure you don't forget any details. It will also give you a skeleton outline to work with. This is definitely my own go-to planning approach. It is also the quickest!

Plan your scene using a 'scene card.' [cwb12.4] This allows you to plan specific details of the scene prior to writing, such as the who, where, when, and what. Once you have this plan in place, the scene is essentially half-written.

Now Write the Full Scene

[cwb12.5] Don't just put flesh on the bones of your plan; write it out from the beginning, focussing on the best words to describe the character and their actions so the reader will visualise the same scene in their minds as you have. Of course, this can be further improved at editing stage.

Scenes should aim to follow the story arc structure, with a beginning, a middle and an end – the same as the overall novel.

Carry on writing a page a day. Use your scene planning techniques to help and keep adhering to or adapting your plans as necessary.

But the number one rule, I must remind you of here is ENJOY YOURSELF! This is the fun bit and you are now working towards your dream – you are writing a novel!

Building Chapters

Firstly, I would suggest that you read this page two or three times. When we 'deconstruct' your novel, as we are about to, it can often provide a lightbulb moment.

Rather than say, the novel being a big, heavy, one slabbed wall, we can break it down into its layers and then break those layers into its bricks and mortar.

As mentioned previously, writing a novel can be likened to a construction project. Some writers write long scenes and call them a chapter. This can make the novel slow, and heavy, and dull.

Some writers write short scenes and describe each one as a 'little chapter.' Whilst this can make for a fast-paced story, it can be disjointed. The best novels combine the two, combining a variety of pace and complexity.

A scene is an episode with a beginning, a middle and an end. A chapter is a series of scenes or episodes which are told sequentially, using the story arc principle (scene setting, rising action, climax, resolution) which moves the novel towards its greater climax. After that comes the resolution of the protagonist's problem or dilemma.

Each chapter is a step along the way. Not always a step forwards. Wonderful story telling involves dealing the protagonist a number of setbacks and allowing the reader to wonder if they will achieve what they are aiming for. This gives us the peaks and troughs of the story. *We will look at this more closely further along in this book in considering tension and pace.*

At the end of each chapter, the reader should have a sense that the chapter has accomplished something – that the story has been enhanced and moved forwards. If chapters do not achieve this, we should give careful thought as to whether they should be included in the overall novel.

The 'mini cliffhanger' at the end of each scene should build towards a slightly bigger cliffhanger at the end of each chapter, perhaps getting bigger as the novel progresses.

Scenes within chapters can be viewed as a series of building blocks; this is repeated over and over again in order to build the book. *Look at a chapter from a book you are presently reading – read it through and see if you can decide where it should be separated into scenes.*

[cwb13.1] ***Now plan the chapter that is coming up next in your novel:***

- What does your protagonist want to achieve over the duration of the chapter?

- What other characters will be in the chapter?
- What conflict will exist in the chapter?

Describe what will happen in:

- Scene one:
- Scene two:
- Scene three:
- Scene four:
- Scene five
- Cliffhanger/ what unanswered question will take the reader into the next chapter?

[cwb13.2] **Further scene development**

You may wish to develop your above scenes further using 'scene cards' or scribble versions, as suggested in the previous section.

This extensive planning process prior to writing may not work for *every* writer for *every* chapter, but can be useful if you are feeling stuck or experiencing a loss of momentum.

It is also handy to have this 'tool' within your writers 'toolbox' for the times when you feel extra planning might be necessary. Sometimes, when a story has taken an unexpected twist whilst I'm writing it, I find I have inadvertently written myself into a 'corner' and something implausible to the reader would have to happen, to get back on track.

At this point, back tracking and planning is needed to navigate around or through this for the story to have integrity.

The more you practice this planning approach, the easier it will come, and remember, if you set off in the dark, you may not arrive, but if you've jotted down some passing places, you've much more chance of making your destination and might also discover some further exciting places along the way.

Keeping it Going

Writing is a solitary activity and all writers suffer a lack of confidence in our work at times, particularly when our writing isn't flowing all that well. Luckily, I find that this is usually temporary and the next day, I'm rolling again! To get those creative juices flowing, does, though, take a conscious effort sometimes.

Having our familiar place to write, set out how we like it, and being there at a consistent time every day all help *get us in the zone.* For those times it doesn't just happen and I feel I would like to get up and do something else, I put the novel aside and write freely about anything else. Before I know it, I'm right back in the zone. Different writing exercises will help you with this, too.

It is vitally important you keep that self-belief and excitement in your novel, after all, if *you* don't believe in what you are doing, then neither will potential publishers or readers.

Your book is *your* brand, it is unique and deserves its place on bookshop shelves amongst all the others. Never lose sight of that.

The other thing to remember is that no one can write your story, other than you. I will probably say that sentence quite a lot in this book!

Writing Affirmations

A powerful exercise is to use a writing affirmation. This is a positive phrase (written in first person, present tense) stating a goal or a truth that you want to impress into your mind. It sounds a bit 'woo-woo,' but trust me, it is really empowering.

The theory is that by clearing your mind and repeating this phrase to yourself out loud, you will create this belief in your conscious mind. A writer might use an affirmation like:

"I am creative and talented" or *"I will keep submitting my work until I am published."*

How Writers Can Use Affirmations

- Keep them brief and limited. Focus on one or two phrases until you feel you've incorporated them into your mind.
- Use the present tense. Instead of *"By next year, I will be famous,"* focus on **today**. *"I have a special gift with words." Or "I can write anything."*
- Say your affirmation to yourself routinely. When you wake up or before you go to sleep. Some people might say them while looking in the mirror and others find that repeating their affirmations during everyday routines, (like a commute or a morning walk) helps them become ingrained.

- Write down your affirmations. You can post them on your computer, stick them on the bathroom mirror, or carry them with you. The act of writing them down and seeing them in print will help fix them in your mind.

[cwb14.1] **Here are some examples of positive affirmations you could use:**

- *I am a writer. Writing is my art.*
- *My wonderful novel will not write itself.*
- *I am creative. My words flow easily.*
- *I write every day and love doing it.*
- *I can visualise success, and I have the patience and talent to reach it.*
- *I can be a successful writer.*
- *No one else can write this novel, but me.* (I told you you'd hear this line again!)

Change your affirmation routinely – maybe once a month.

Go on, give it a try – even if you feel a bit sceptical.

[cwb14.2] **At this point in your writing, it is a great time to consider the following:**

1. At what point are you at in your novel? (*Word count, percentage, chapter)*
2. What has happened so far? *(How far have you got along the storyline?)*
3. What has yet to happen? (*How far have you got to go?)*

4. What could happen now that could blow everything apart? Can you pose any 'what ifs' to your novel? (*Something that could change the whole direction of your novel – just some ideas, you don't have to run with any of them)*
5. How would I feel if I gave up on it now? *Around a quarter of the way through is the danger zone for many first time novelists – don't be one of them!*
6. How will I feel when I hold the proof of my novel in my hands? *Keeping your thoughts on the end result can be empowering and motivating.*

You can keep revisiting these questions; as you progress, your responses will change. Hopefully, after this session, and after the formation of your writing affirmation, you will be feeling empowered. Keep going – you're doing great!

Development of Story

OK, so this section of the book contrasts slightly with the previous one. But this point in your novel, is the prime time for getting into a tangle. I'm here to help you stop this from happening! If you are mindful of 'writing traps' you can fall into, then you can ensure you avoid them as you continue to write your novel.

[cwb15.1] **From those listed below, choose the one you feel is causing you the most concern and then follow the advice given.** Please only choose one!

This is by no means an exhaustive list, but they are some of the common plot 'pitfalls' with ways for you to remedy them.

Originality of Plot. *Are you worried you might be 'regurgitating' something you might have once read in another book or seen in a movie?*

Step back from your work and identify the similar 'original' work. Make a list of ideas going backwards and forwards, of how you can ensure it will differ from its 'lookalike.'

These ideas do not have to be anything major or drastic. Coming up with them can help you detach from unintentional imitation. Remember, though, that most tropes and scenarios *have* been done before, to some extent. But *no one* has created *your* characters, *your* setting, and *your* plot.

Predictability of Plot. *Are you concerned that readers will be able to tell very early on how your book will unfold?*

Return to your plan and re-read your story so far. Can you identify the overriding issue, problem or obstacle of the story? Have you inadvertently given solutions and answers away? Are clues you have already planted too obvious?

Try to surprise your readers. You need more than one or two suspects if writing crime, or potential outcomes for other genres. Drop subtle clues for each one as the story progresses. This is probably the plot pitfall that I worry about the most, especially as I am a crime writer. But it is easily remedied, trust me.

Interest of Plot. *Will your plot be absorbing and exciting for your readers?*

This is a pitfall I think most writers worry about, particularly at first draft stage. Do you have a scene or chapter that is necessary to take your story forward, but you don't feel is as *interesting* as other scenes in your novel? The good news is, this is also an easy problem to sort out.

Firstly, can you imagine what different writers might do with it? How would the comedy writer write it? A mystery writer? A horror writer? Secondly, pose a *'what if.'* Imagine the most surprising thing that could happen in a scene or chapter. One of these ideas might fit your story.

Action-Packed Plot. *Is your story too fast and busy?*

Let your reader breathe from time to time. Give them a little downtime now and then. Use conversations, summarised passages, meals, introspection and releases of emotions that are set in between the car chases, shootouts and confrontations to achieve this. Similarly, you may have the opposite problem where your narrative feels a little slow. We will soon come to the section on 'pace,' which will help you balance this problem out.

Complex Plot. Are you getting 'bogged down' in detail?

Often, a complex scene or chapter can be trimmed into a sleeker one. To find messiness in an overly complex scene, summarise it out loud to yourself. If it takes too long to explain, ask yourself:

"Why does s/he do/say that? Why didn't s/he just do/say this?" Can something be explained through a character's thoughts or speech instead of lots of description? I find that this is often best sorted out at editing stage but it is a very common pitfall to fall into, we writers often try to say too much, when we can say far less and let the reader do some work.

Shallow Plot. *Are you more caught up in the writing than the story itself?*

This refers to the metaphors, dialogue and descriptions, instead of *plot*. Sometimes we ride these skills over the surface of the story and forget what's really important.

If you sense that the novel feels insubstantial, step back and ask yourself: Why am I writing this story? Why does the outcome matter to the characters? How do the characters change throughout the story? Considering these questions will afford your story more depth.

Remember that the first draft stage is *you telling the story to yourself.* It's more important to keep your focus on the plot at this stage than the writing techniques. You can pay more attention to these at second draft stage.

Inauthentic, unbelievable plot. *Are you concerned that your story is becoming too far-fetched for your reader to remain engaged?*

Readers need to buy into the reality put forward by what they are reading. You may go too far with a plot or not far enough. Even with fantasy and science fiction, there needs to be an 'element' of possibility and plausibility, to keep your reader hooked in. A second opinion later on will help you with this.

Too many sub-plots. *Are you struggling to keep track of everything as the writer?*

Then so will the reader. If you start to feel weighed down by your numerous storylines, consider trimming some of them. You risk losing your reader if they have to keep flicking back to check names, places, facts, etc.

List the subplots and then list under each one, all the ways they are necessary, and how they add something to your overall story. If the story would remain strong without them, that is probably the biggest hint that you can afford to lose them.

We should keep only subplots that are so vital that you could not remove them without destroying your novel. Similarly, if you only have the main plot line, and no sub plots, this is something you will need to revisit. Sub plots are derived from the goals of your secondary characters.

Illogical Sequence. *Are you feeling that the order of scenes, events or chapters in your story is 'off?'*

Sometimes the sequence set down in an outline shows its true colours when you're writing the chapters.

List each scene on a post it note, then think about moving them around into a different order. However, it doesn't matter if you jump forwards or backwards through the narrative or use a storytelling device known as 'flashback,' as long as you make this clear to the reader. If you don't, then you risk losing them.

Mediocre Premise of Plot. *Will the basis of your story make readers curious? Can you describe the foundation of your story? Have you clearly defined, early on, what is at stake? (e.g. freedom, reputation.)*

Have a think about where you might make the stakes higher, the characters more emotional, the setting more atmospheric. The last thing you want your reader to think is, 'so what.'

Now return to the plan you wrote.

[cwb15.2] **Make a list of the key moments in your story** when something major happens – the main plot points which your novel hangs on.

[cwb15.3] **Is there anything you could do to provide more depth to them?** For example, how could an event affect an additional character. If it's something adverse that is happening, could it be made even worse? Could two things happen in quick succession?

A brilliant story can be about the reader wondering just how much more a character can take and this will be returned to in the section about creating tension.

Please don't be downhearted at the mention of all these potential pitfalls, especially when I have brought it to you, hot on the heels of the 'believing in yourself' section. I have fallen into each and every one of these pitfalls but often haven't identified them until much later. You're aware of them now, which means you can do something about it!

Viewpoint

'Viewpoint' is sometimes confused with 'voice.'

To remember which is which, it is helpful to take a 'cinematic' approach. I also find this really exciting, I mean, who doesn't want to imagine their very own novel being acted out on the big screen, or even the small screen, with their favourite actor taking the lead role?

Viewpoint is determined by how a character has the camera *on* them or *from* them. So, they may be holding the camera themselves, the camera might be 'behind their eyes,' or someone else entirely may have hold of the camera.

The camera may shift around but will be clearly focused on one of the following viewpoints: first, second, third, multiple or omniscient. (If confused do not worry… see below.)

Voice is determined by the choice of character to *tell* the story and how this choice colours the way it is told from the character's personality, backstory, accent, experience, etc. We looked at this previously.

The main viewpoints available to writers are:

First-Person (I/me)

Where the 'camera' looks through the eyes of a single character, usually the protagonist. Only events that this character witnesses can be reported through the narrative.

In contemporary fiction, sometimes more than one first-person viewpoint is used. It needs to be made very clear to the reader, whose viewpoint they are in at that point in the story, to avoid confusion.

This is where 'voice' intertwines with 'viewpoint;' as when using more than one viewpoint, the voices of the characters must be distinct from one another.

There would usually be no more than two viewpoint characters and this approach would normally only work where there is merit in hearing from two characters equally. The duration of a character's viewpoint is usually a whole chapter.

Advantage: First-person viewpoint creates immediacy and intimacy with the reader and involves them more directly. It can build suspense as the reader only knows what the protagonist knows, making it easy for the author to deliberately withhold information and then spring a 'surprise.'

Disadvantage: Nothing can happen without the viewpoint character. This can be restrictive.

Example

I'm pleased to find he's still on it. He's got steaks in the pan and two large glasses of red are waiting on the table. I take a large sip from one, then set about finding some candles.

"Candles! What do we want candles for?" He laughs as I light them. "Are we planning a power cut?"

Second Person (you)

Where the narrator/character addresses either the reader directly or another character in the story, as though they are listening/reading.

It is a lesser used viewpoint, but can be effective and engaging if done well and consistently. The narrator/character still has the camera behind their eyes, but they're pointing it directly at the reader.

Advantage: It is an original and innovative way of narrating a book which can help make it stand out amongst its competitors.

Disadvantage: It is hard to maintain throughout an entire novel. With readers often finding it intrusive, as it can feel as though the author is addressing them directly.

Example

You're uncharacteristically early and the first person I notice when I step through the heavy wooden doors, fifteen minutes before the service is due to begin.

I want to thump you when I see what you're wearing. Trackies. Hoody. Trainers. You never did have any respect for her, did you?

Third-Person (single viewpoint) (he/she)

Technically, the same as first person, the main difference is in the pronoun and the effect being less intimate and less confessional.

As in first person, this viewpoint can be shifted, as long as it is clear when it is being changed. The narrator still has the 'camera' but instead of it being behind their eyes, it's as though it's being carried on their shoulder.

There are usually no more than two viewpoint characters, and the consideration should be: is there merit in following two characters equally?

The duration of a viewpoint is usually an entire chapter and can then alternate between the two characters, chapter by chapter.

Example

"It would have been quicker to walk." Ellen dug her fingers into her bag and sat forwards. "Excuse me," she muttered to the lady next to her.

"You can't get off here," the driver said. "We're at the lights."

"Watch me." Ellen pressed the emergency exit button and jumped onto the pavement, breaking into a run as her kitten heels made contact with the concrete.

The advantages and disadvantages would be similar to those when using first person narrative.

Third-Person (multiple viewpoint) (he/she)

In this form, viewpoint shifts from character to character. The reader is privy to the thoughts of all characters but with no authorial knowledge outside the characters' own. It is wise to limit the number of viewpoints used and to make it very clear when it changes.

Usually a change of scene is used for each viewpoint scene. It is as though the camera is being passed from character to character.

Advantage: It is easier for the author to tell the story

Disadvantage: It is harder for the reader to become emotionally involved with a particular character and can also be confusing.

Example

They stride away from the renewed frenzy, amidst further flashing bulbs. Paul feels an unfamiliar jauntiness to his step for the first time in a long time. He never has to see that place again.

"He's been acquitted. He's sat here with his first pint. Why don't you come over?" Alana speaks guardedly into her phone to Lee, not wanting Paul to hear. "It looks bad that you don't appear to have taken an interest and you won't wish him well."

Omniscient Narrator or 'God's Eye View'

An 'all-seeing, all-knowing' narrative view where the viewpoint not only shifts from character to character but into the narration as well. This enables general overviews to be provided or the possibility of going off on digressionary asides but then to zoom back in close. It is as though the camera is up in the air, above the 'stage.'

Advantage: It is versatile and flexible in terms of storytelling and conveying information.

Disadvantage: It distances the reader from identification with the characters as it is an objective and impersonal viewpoint. It is little used in contemporary fiction and regarded as old-fashioned.

Example

"Why are you sleeping here Daddy?" Emily was surprised to find her father asleep on the sofa.

"Ssssh, sweetheart. Mummy's sleeping." Paul yawned as he sat up. "We don't want to wake her up." It didn't feel like five minutes since he's fallen asleep. He felt exhausted.

"Can I open the curtains Daddy?" She bounced towards the window. "Let the sunshine in?" She liked it when it was just her and her dad. Their neighbour, happy to see Emily, smiled at her from the garden next door.

Michelle jumped out of bed, angry that they had woken her up. "For God's sake!"

Perhaps you can identify novels you have read, which exemplify when each viewpoint has been used.

Consider what viewpoint you are using in your own novel? Can you explain why you chose it or is it what felt most comfortable as you set off writing?

[cwb16.1] **An Experiment with Viewpoint**

Read through a scene you have recently written.

If you've written in first-person viewpoint, try changing it into third or vice versa. Compare the ease of writing to that when you originally wrote it. How does the piece differ? Often, as readers, we have a preference, so this, like many other aspects of narrative, might transfer into our writing style.

[cwb16.2] **Second Person Narration**

Have a practice at writing in second person. *It's more difficult than it seems!*

Write a scene where your character is taking a journey of some description and is addressing a character who isn't actually with them. Use 'you' language throughout. Here is another example of this viewpoint being used:

This car suited you, but it's too 'girly' for me. I do feel as though I'm doing something wrong, driving it, but if it's not driven, it will seize up or something. I really think I'll flog it, though I'm not ready to yet. You lent me it a few times after I first passed my test when you didn't need it. "Look after it," you would say.

Building Narrative

To be sure....!!

'Narrator' is *the voice telling the story* (incorporating interior voice which we will return to soon.)

'Narrative' is *the story being told.*

'Narration' is a combination of the above.

Good storytelling relies on the 'seamless interweaving' of the elements below:

- Setting
- Back Story
- Character Action
- Interiority
- Dialogue

This is easier said than done but the good news is, like every aspect of being a writer, it gets easier with the more writing that you do. (I promise!)

Read the following example scene, followed by the notes afterwards which look at the elements necessary to create a compelling narrative.

"My name is DC Joseph Calvert, interviewing officer. For the benefit of the tape, can you both state your full names?"

"Paul Alan Jackson." Paul grips the table between them. This is surreal. He can't believe where he is. Any moment he will wake up to find Emily and his dog bounding into the bedroom.

DC Calvert then nods to his colleague. "DC Alan Whittaker."

"DC Whittaker is attending in a note-taking capacity." DC Calvert turns towards Paul. "Can you confirm you do not wish to have a solicitor present?"

"No, I don't." Paul clears his throat. "I want to get this over with and get myself to the hospital." He glances around the confining green walls, ignoring the nagging voice that says you need a solicitor, you idiot. His work colleague, John, who is a solicitor, is going to kill him for this.

"OK, well, as I've already outlined, you're free to leave at any time, you're not under arrest at this stage. You also have the right to request a solicitor; if you decide to exercise this right, we will simply stop the interview. However, you are being interviewed under caution, this interview is being recorded, and I must remind you of your rights." He pauses for a sharp intake of breath. "You have the right to remain silent but anything you do say can and may be used as evidence against you. Do you understand your rights or do you need them explaining to you?"

"I understand." Paul has heard them often enough on the TV. He feels dizzy again. His anxiety levels and the temperature of the room are conspiring against him. He hopes he can hold up and get this over with.

Setting An airless and confining interview room within a police station. There is a table between the protagonist and the two interviewing male officers. The room is brightly lit with fluorescent lighting and has no window. There is a camera in the corner and a voice recording device positioned on a shelf on the wall. The furniture is all fastened to the floor and is dark green. The room has a musty smell and a claustrophobic feel.

Back Story Paul is about to be interviewed in a local police station about events leading up to the discovery of his badly injured wife in their holiday cottage the day before. His wife is fighting for her life in hospital and his daughter is being cared for by her grandmother. They were heard rowing the previous day by neighbouring cottages. He has spent the night in custody.

Character Action Paul is gripping the table with anxiety. DC Whittaker is taking notes and DC Calvert is conducting the interview. DC Calvert starts the tape and Paul clears his throat, ready to speak before looking around at his surroundings.

Interiority Paul can't believe where he is and recalls the day before when Emily and his dog came bounding into his room. A voice nags at him to ring his work colleague who is a solicitor. He starts to feel dizzy due to his anxiety and the heat of the room and hopes he can maintain his composure for the duration of the interview.

Dialogue "My name is DC Joseph Calvert, interviewing officer. For the benefit of the tape, can you both state your full names?"

"Paul Oliver Jackson."

"DC Alan Whittaker."

"DC Whittaker is attending in a note-taking capacity. Can you confirm that you do not wish to have a solicitor present?"

"No, I don't."

"OK. Well, as I've already outlined, you're free to leave at any time – you're not under arrest at this stage. You have the right to request a solicitor; if you decide to exercise this right, we will simply stop the interview..."

[cwb17.1] **Your turn! Bring to mind the next scene you plan to write and make notes under the following headings:**

1. Setting: *Where is the scene set? Use all the senses, as always. Remember that smell is particularly provocative.*
2. Back Story: *What has brought the characters to where they are now? What has gone before should be 'drip fed' through a narrative.*
3. Character Action: *What are the characters doing?*
4. Interiority: *What is the viewpoint character thinking?*
5. Dialogue: *What are the characters saying to each other?*

Within all this, ensure you are conveying something of feeling and emotion – remember, this is what nurtures the connection between the reader and your characters.

[cwb17.2] **Now write your scene**, aiming for a seamless 'interweaving' of these narrative elements as you write.

Keep these principles in mind as you continue your novel. You won't nail this until later drafts, but if you've got it in mind at first or second draft stage, you will be in a stronger position when editing.

Narrative Interiority

The last section looked at the components that make up a 'narrative;' dialogue, setting, backstory, action and ***internal thought***.

A character's 'thinking' can add power and depth to your writing. This is known as 'internal thought' or 'narrative interiority.' It is as powerful as the use of dialogue, and as a writer, I love using it and is one of the primary tools in my writing toolbox.

This is because of the *emotional connection* that is created from being privy to a character's internal thoughts. It is extremely effective when you are using first person narrative.

Below is a scene where internal thought has been used in the narrative. Can you identify the instances where the character is thinking to himself?

When the viewpoint character is *thinking* something, their thought is placed at the side of something they are *saying* or *doing*. Extra emphasis on a thought, can be shown through using italics.

Calvert runs his finger down a sheet of paper. "You arrived back two hours and twenty minutes before you made the three nines call to the police?"

"Yes, that sounds about right." Paul is too exhausted to work this out clearly. He must stay focused. He hopes he's saying the right things.

"What happened in that time? The two hours and twenty minutes."

Paul hesitates. "Michelle was groggy and grumpy, she always is when she's had a drink earlier in the day." He can never do anything much to appease her when she's in that sort of a mood.

"How do you know this?"

What a stupid question. Talk about asking the obvious. "I've been with her for ten years. I know when she's in a bad mood. She shouted at me for not waking her earlier."

"Then what happened?"

"At her request, we sent Emily to bed, and I was chopping salad up for dinner." Paul rubs at his eyes. They are burning with exhaustion. What he wouldn't give to turn the clock back.

[cwb18.1] **Bring your main character to mind.** The following scenarios may or may not make it into your novel but they will get you into the head of your main character and in turn, help you get to know him or her even better than you do already.

What thought (just one line) was, or may have been, going through their head when:

1. They were opening an envelope (or about to take a call) with some test results.
2. They were walking into their first day at a new job. (or other new situation)

3. Someone was ringing them who they really didn't want to speak with.
4. A time they were trying to think up an excuse as to why they were late.
5. A store assistant was telling them the price of something they couldn't afford.
6. A family member was accusing them of something they had not done.
7. They bumped into an ex partner.

[cwb18.2] **Build a scene from one of these responses,** ensuring an interweaving of narrative elements; dialogue, action, setting and back story, whilst paying attention to your viewpoint character's internal thought.

Remember, you can only know what your viewpoint characters are thinking – you cannot know what any of the other characters' thoughts are. I think this is an important distinction. As a reader, I have been put off continuing with a book when the author is accidently slipping into the thoughts of a non-viewpoint character.

As you write your scene, keep pulling in all the areas of narrative, but with your focus on internal thought. It could be helpful to look at how other authors achieve the writing of internal thought by looking at a chapter of a novel.

Again, I remind you to keep reading. Along with this book, and your own writing practice, the act of reading will be your greatest teacher.

And speaking of writing practice, keep going! At least a page every day, if you can. Even if you don't feel overly happy at its first draft appearance, there'll be plenty of chance to make it better soon.

Letting Readers do the Work

Reading is an active process, where the story lives within a reader's imagination. Where they can hear our character's voices and visualise them, and their surroundings.

Our readers should also be enabled to make inferences from a story instead of being 'spoon-fed' every piece of information. This idea extends the 'show don't tell' concept, from a previous section; *what is not said can be as powerful as what is said.*

In a novel, description and detail turn into *images* in a reader's mind. But too much can be distracting and overwhelming. Every author has a distinct style, usually honed over time.

Ernest Hemingway was known for short, declarative sentences devoid of flowery description. One of his most famous stories is this seemingly simple six-word story:

'For sale, baby shoes, never worn.'

[cwb19.1] **What might be the story behind these six words?**

If you're anything like me, you will immediately allow your imagination to take over, and fill in the backstory behind this tale.

At the other end of the spectrum, Charles Dickens used 'profuse linguistic creativity' in his work. Consider this passage from *The Old Curiosity Shop*:

The town was glad with morning light; places that had shown ugly and distrustful all night long, now wore a smile; and sparkling sunbeams dancing on chamber windows, and twinkling through blind and curtains before sleepers' eyes, shed light even into dreams, and chased away the shadows of the night.

Birds in hot rooms, covered up close and dark, felt it was morning, and chafed and grew restless in their little cells; bright-eyed mice crept back to their tiny homes and nestled timidly together; the sleek house-cat, forgetful of her prey, sat winking at the rays of sun starting through keyhole and cranny in the door, and longed for her stealthy run and warm sleek bask outside.

[cwb19.2] **Pick out the key information and condense the passage into no more than twenty-five words. Can you then break it down into six?**

Balancing the Two

Whichever style *you* prefer is a personal preference; although some readers might argue that Dickens' description of the town is too detailed and leaves nothing to the imagination, whilst other readers might like the poetic and evocative description.

However you feel about the styles of Dickens or Hemingway, there is something to be said for finding the *middle ground*: enough description to fire your reader's imagination, but not so much in order that the story drowns in detail.

[cwb19.3] **As you are writing your next scene**, consider whether you're allowing the reader the freedom to create a vivid picture in their mind, or whether you're giving them too much information.

If it is the latter, you are in danger of *doing their job for them* — instead, keep in mind that the best stories are a *collaboration* between writer and reader.

As a reader of thrillers, there is nothing like a *whodunnit* to enable me to do some work but I also like to make more general story inferences too. One way of doing this is to allow 'pauses' between chapters where the reader can infer some more, without having to be told, what might be going on 'behind the scenes.'

This approach allows the author to avoid mundanity within the narrative and instead draw the reader into more exciting and interesting events.

[cwb19.4] **Have a look through your own chapter endings and new chapter beginnings** in your novel so far, and decide whether you are allowing space and time to elapse between a chapter's end and the beginning of a new one, where a reader can be left to deduce what is going on.

I accept that to have this in mind at first draft stage is a challenge so don't get too hung up on it but once you are editing, keep asking yourself, *is this something I need to 'tell' the reader, or am I already 'showing' it to them.*

Creating a Strong Story – Pace and Tension

I will now talk about two more important tools to have in your writer's toolbox – pace and tension. Both are essential to keep your reader turning the pages.

Maintaining a Strong Story Using Pace

Pace plays an important role in narrative. With effective use of it, we can keep the reader on the edge of their seat before being offered a reprieve. This determines whether they will continue to read or put the book down.

Definition

Narrative pace determines how quickly or how slowly the writer takes a reader through a story. It relies on a combination of mood and emotion as these elements play out in the dialogue, setting and action.

For example, a story such as Dan Brown's "The DaVinci Code" has a much faster pace than Elizabeth Gilbert's "Eat, Pray, Love." The pace of any story should vary; the opening pace may feel different from that of the story's climax.

Upping the Pace

Fast action and rapid sequencing can put a little spring into the narrative's step, as can a cliffhanger. Both of these narrative elements make the reader want to go on to the next page to see what happens to the story's protagonist.

Action sequences containing little dialogue and few internal thoughts from the characters best create this feeling. Using short transitions in between scenes works in conjunction with the action sequences to get the story moving.

Also related to these literary devices is the use of rapid sequencing. If big plot moments happen one right after the other, the pace of the novel feels faster. Shorter chapters also increase the pace of a story.

Slowing It Down

Narrative passages that contain a great deal of detail, slowly establishing scenes and containing longer sentences, feel slower than other parts of the story. Additionally, writing longer chapters or switching the narrative's focus to another subplot conveys a passage of time. These elements bring the pace down, building suspense and allowing the reader to catch their breath between action sequences.

Striking a Balance

The most interesting stories contain sequences that move at different speeds. These keep the reader engaged. Juxtaposing chapters that feature mostly dialogue alongside others which impart information and interspersing them with fast-paced action sequences can strike the right balance.

[cwb20.1] **Write a scene in which your character is on their way somewhere – write it at a *fast pace.***

1. Quick action and fast to read.
2. 'Strong' verbs – thump, swing, march, drag.
3. Minimal dialogue.
4. Short sentences.
5. Action rather than description.

[cwb20.2] **Then write a scene in which your character is leaving that place – write it at a *slow pace.***

1. Longer sentences.
2. Scene setting.
3. Description.
4. Internal thoughts.
5. Emotions expressed are sadness and loneliness.
6. Softer verbs – tuck, tug, fumble.

I will now talk about how you can create and sustain tension throughout your story. Without 'tension' there is no novel!

Set up the tension.

Keep saying *no* to your characters. Whatever it is they want, *hold it back.* The best conflict is one that appears unsolvable, so pile difficult situations on your characters and make them prove themselves. Don't make their situations easier; always make their lives harder. Put as many obstacles as possible in their way.

Look at your character's goals, and ask yourself, "What's the worst thing that could happen?" Then take that worst thing a step further. For increased emotional intensity, conflict should directly relate to your character's internal goals *and* to their backstory.

Make the reader feel the emotions along with your characters.

It doesn't matter what kind of book you're writing or who your characters are - *a story is about feelings.* The more that is at stake for your character, the more emotions he or she feels about events and situations, the more a reader will engage with them–but they must be enabled to *care.*

If you've set up your character for a big problem, be ready to fire it at him. Internal and external conflict and character motivation *must* be in place to create tension.

Use your character's *internal* conflict to its best advantage: abandonment, mistrust, emotional deprivation, dependence, social exclusion, or whatever vulnerability you create. You now must use those conflicts and fatal flaws in the scene to challenge readers to keep reading and, most importantly, to keep them caring. If you as the writer can feel the emotion, you can convey it effectively to the reader.

Change is also what keeps the reader turning pages. New challenges, new information, new twists, and added complications—all must be assumed and planned for by you the writer, ahead of time, so that your story has the potential for tension.

[cwb20.3] **Write a scene in which something goes wrong for your character.** Have your character facing a conflict; a situation that appears as though something cannot be achieved or a problem that cannot be solved.

Then go back through it, adding more things that could go wrong. A scene in which everything can go wrong, does go wrong, will serve to increase the tension in your scene and have the reader routing for your character.

The Climax of your Novel

The 'climax' of a book (also known as the peak, culmination or pinnacle,) should be the *highest* point of your story. It occurs shortly before the ending (the resolution,) which we will be also looking at in the next section.

To be effective, your climax scenes need to embody the following qualities:

- It should be a moment in time that has been built towards, near the end of the story.
- As many of the characters as possible, should be affected at this point. This is where you will bring any sub plots in line with your main plot.
- As a consequence of this heightened tension, an emotional effect will be placed upon the reader.
- How the story will end should not be obvious – the reader will hopefully be guessing. I would say you should have them on the edge of their seat!!

Think of a novel you have recently read. Write some notes on what the 'peak' point was and whether it was done effectively.

Even if you are nowhere near the actual writing of your climatic scene yet, planning ahead will increase your focus and direction.

Your readers should have a *general* idea of what's coming (thanks to your effective foreshadowing,) and there is no way they should be considering putting the book down at his stage. This is where you want them to keep turning the pages into the early hours.

They should be asking: *What's going to happen? Is the main character going to survive? Will he save the world/his family/the battle/his life in time?* Or whatever else is at stake for your main and secondary characters.

[cwb21.1] **The following questions may help you to plan this part of your novel:**

1. *What has been the overall main goal/quest of your central character within your novel? Try to be specific.*
2. *What obstacle has been getting in the way of this?*
3. *What needs to happen for the goal to be achieved?*
4. *How differently would your story end if the 'obstacle' was to win out?*
5. *What emotions will be experienced by the characters at this point?*
6. *How close to the end is this moment going to occur?*

[cwb21.2] **Draft a scene or two from the climax of your story.**

This is not 'set in stone' and can be changed if need be. You will find that it supports the novel's direction.

Whilst looking ahead, keep going with your ongoing writing a page every day. Keep those words coming and resist the temptation to edit them. We're coming to that very soon!

The Resolution of your Story

The resolution (also known as the ending or conclusion,) happens at the very end of your book. It begins directly after the climax and continues until the last page. A resolution can vary in length, but, generally speaking, shorter is better.

The story is essentially over, and there is no need to tie off every loose end perfectly. You can 'pave the way' for a sequel which, in turn, will make your book a more prospective proposition for publishers.

The length of your resolution will depend on a couple of factors, the most important being the number of remaining loose ends – this can be linked to the number of 'sub-plots' you have had going on.

Optimally, you will have used the scenes leading up to your climax to tie off as many of these as possible, which will free up your resolution to take care of only the essentials. To be effective, it should embody the following qualities:

1. It will answer any of the reader's remaining unanswered questions.

2. It should leave the reader feeling in a particular way, (sad, optimistic, etc.)
3. It might carry a message.

[cwb22.1] **Think of a book you have been recently reading** and jot some notes down on why you think its resolution was done effectively. A good ending will stay with the reader for a long time.

The other factor to keep in mind is the *tone* with which you want to leave your readers. You want them to be recommending your book to everyone they know! This is your last chance to influence their perception of your story. So consider how you want to end things. Happy? Sad? Thoughtful? Funny?

[cwb22.2] **Jot down responses to the following prompts:**

- *What loose ends will you need to tie up between the climatic part of the story and the resolution?*
- *Will any unanswered questions remain in the mind of the reader?*
- *What emotion do you want them to be left with?*
- *Is a sequel in any way possible, based on your ending? This could be a continuation of the story, a spinoff or a similarity in theme or character.*
- *What is the key lesson you want the reader to take from your story? What is its message?*

[cwb22.3] ***Now, plan and write a first draft of your resolution***

Even if you are nowhere near the actual writing of your ending yet, many writers I have worked with report that planning and first drafting their ending in advance supports their sense of direction.

And enjoy this bit! With the climax and resolution roughly in place, you can now really see where you are going – exciting stuff!

Tightening Writing

I promised that we would get around to having a look at editing, so here we are – starting with *tightening* your writing.

Some writers see the creative process as the most fun part of writing a novel but I have, over time, grown to love the editing stage of producing a novel too. To use an analogy, it can be likened to taking a precious jewel and polishing it until it shines.

Unnecessary words and phrases can easily find their way into our writing and drag it down. We should aim to write as concisely as possible for our *meaning* to be understood. It's not all that difficult to do and shouldn't affect your writing style or voice.

The key is not to cut and tighten *everything* that ***could*** be tightened, but to examine whether keeping, discarding, or adding an adverb or adjective best conveys your intent for the sentence in as few words as possible.

Eliminate superfluous words Make a list of these. The pesky words you throw in out of habit like *very, just, so* and *quite*. Or phrases like *began to,* or *started to.* Print a random page of your novel and see if you can weed out at least one or two words from every sentence. It may not be possible, but it is a valuable exercise. If a word does not add importance to a sentence, it should go. Do this throughout your novel at the editing stage.

Avoid being too wordy. Don't use two words when one will say the same thing. Don't use four when three will do. If two adjectives are similar, pick the best one and lose the other.

Lose the speech tags. If you are writing fiction or narrative nonfiction, you need to have dialogue in your story. If the reader knows who is speaking, you do not need to keep telling them—especially in a scene with only two characters. And remove all those flowery verbs that stick out, such as *quizzed, extrapolated, exclaimed,* and *interjected.* They can 'jar' a reader out of a story. Just use *said* and *asked,* and maybe an occasional *replied* or *answered.*

And a word about backstory Look at all the incidences of backstory and reduce to a few lines of the most important information that the reader *must* know to "get" the story. Can a character either think or say these things instead of going into lengthy description?

Example of an 'overwritten' piece that could be 'tightened.'

Derek, a tall, greying gentleman in his middle age, felt mildly disappointed and a little bit rejected that no one, in the room whatsoever, seemed to have remembered his fifty-seventh birthday.

He looked quizzically at his balding, middle-aged friend George and started to wonder if he had possibly said anything to maybe deter his friends and acquaintances that it was, in fact, his birthday.

Maybe George, who was getting a bit forgetful these days, had actually failed to remember as well?

[cwb23.1] **Rewrite the above passage, taking the 'tightening writing' advice into consideration.**

[cwb23.2] **Then select a chapter you have written, to experiment with tightening your own writing.**

This process should not usually be undertaken until your first draft is complete, but because this is a necessary part of your writing skill development, concentrate on an earlier section of your novel which will have 'gone cold' due to the time which has elapsed since you initially drafted it.

Print your chosen chapter in double line spacing so you have plenty of room for annotations.

Editing

As previously mentioned, ideally the editing process should not be carried out when initially drafting your work.

The first draft is *you,* telling yourself the story and like I have mentioned before, is often considered as the fun, creative process. You need to get your story and thoughts and ideas down first. There is no need to concentrate on spelling, layout or punctuation until the editing stage.

Below is the 'process' I use from the planning to the publication stage, leaving a period of time, (at least a few days,) in between the latter stages.

Allowing some time in between edits allows you to see your story with 'fresh eyes.'

1. Ideas, notes and planning of scenes, chapters and story.
2. First draft.
3. Typing your handwritten draft, improving throughout. Taking bits out or adding things in.
4. Going back over this work and improving again. (Using the checklist in this section.) *If you have worked straight*

onto a computer, stages three and four may be combined.

5. Printing out and annotating with a pen. *You will see things on the page, that you would miss on the screen.*
6. Taking these amendments back to the computer.
7. Reading through, making more adjustments.
8. Reading aloud. *It's amazing how many errors reveal themselves here!*
9. Final proofread.
10. Someone else reading it. (Another writer, working in the same genre as you, can be an excellent choice.)

The final stages are less time intensive than the earlier ones, but all are of equal importance.

Your editing checklist, concentrating on a section of the novel at a time:

- Decide whether your novel has started in the right place. Writers often start too early, giving too much explanation or backstory first rather than going straight in at a point of action.
- Know what your novel is trying to achieve, its message, its journey. Has it been successful in doing this?
- Check every word is the best it can be. Use a thesaurus to help. Or the 'synonyms' function on your computer. Every word counts.
- Beware of 'overwriting.' Of being too wordy. Less is often more so go easy with the adjectives – see previous section on tightening your writing.
- Consistency, with regards to viewpoint, character details, etc.

- Remember that reading should be an active process – enable the reader to 'fill in gaps' themselves where possible.
- Ensure you're showing rather than telling.
- Search and get rid of repetition. We often repeat words, phrases, or ideas in the same paragraph.
- Beware of redundancies, e.g. *"a cacophony of sound," "combine together,"* and *"commute back and forth."* Examine each word you use. Omit needless words.
- Have someone else read your work. Ask them to consider:

Were they sure of the location? Were they certain which character was doing the talking and feeling? Another reader can offer invaluable feedback on where you need to bolster your descriptions to aid the reader's comprehension.

- Editing does not just mean 'cutting' things out – bits that you've 'skipped over' may also need expansion.

An example of an underwritten piece which needs expansion

It was a lovely sunny day but something was definitely brewing. He had been in a bad mood before he went out and now she was trying to keep busy before his return.

She'd already been on the phone to her friend who had invited her to get out of the way and stay with her but she had thought that she had better stay and face the music.

She found herself remembering all the things that had been happening lately and this just made her more anxious.

Finally, he came back, and they had a massive argument. She ended up having to sleep in the spare room.

[cwb24.1] **How could this piece of writing be expanded and improved?**

[cwb24.2] **Re-write the scene, using your ideas.**

Typesetting, Presentation and Perfecting your Manuscript

Your submission package to publishers will be composed of three elements:

- The covering letter
- The first three chapters
- The overall synopsis

It is essential that your first three chapters, (and the rest of your novel,) along with your cover letter and synopsis is professionally presented. I will cover the required content of your cover letter and synopsis in forthcoming sections.

Publishers and literary agents are hugely busy people and whilst they're looking for wonderful, saleable stories, they're also looking for an excuse to reject a manuscript straightaway, thus reducing their 'to read' pile. Don't let presentation prevent you getting over the first hurdle!

Look at some published books to get a sense of layout, line indents, paragraph spacing, etc. Some publishers may differ slightly in their requirements, and I advise you to check these and follow them closely. And, if you follow the guidance below, which deals with the presentation of your work, you will be giving it the best chance.

First, you must include an overall cover sheet detailing your name and contact information, the book title, genre and word count.

Chapter Headings

Make sure these are consistent throughout your novel, in terms of whether they are emboldened, underlined, CAPITALISED or centred.

If numbering your chapters, they should either be consistently numbers (1,2...) or consistently words (one, two...) throughout.

Font

Make sure the font is legible, (12 point is usual,) and consistent throughout your novel, use Aerial or Times New Roman. Text should be double spaced and left aligned (not justified.)

Margins

Standard margin size on A4 is 2.54cm on all sides.

Presentation

All pages should be numbered. Furthermore, they should all have a header set, (in a smaller font size than the main text,) that gives the author name and the book title in italics.

Layout

Read this bit very carefully. When I go over this in my face to face writing course sessions, I always get a few puzzled faces... to start with!

Paragraphs do not need a gap between them. Only leave a space if there is a change of scene. There is no need to use * to indicate a scene break unless it occurs at the top or bottom of a page.

Never indent the first line in a new chapter or the first line after a scene break. But the beginning of every paragraph should be indented. This includes paragraphs that consist of dialogue.

Quality of Printed Work (If submitting by hard copy)

Don't print your work off when your printer is running out of ink or has problems. Faint or mis-coloured text, or text with horizontal or missing lines, is difficult to read and therefore unlikely to be considered.

Print on one side of white plain A4 paper only. It is fairly unusual for publishers to request hard copy these days, but always double check!

[cwb25.1] **Go through your manuscript,** whatever stage you are at, checking it is presented as above.

Creating an On-Line Author Platform

An author platform has two elements; the *offline* one which comprises real, physical writing communities, you can take part in, such as writing circles or literary events you attend. We will look at this more closely in the next section.

Then there's the *online* element, which comprises social media, blogging and having a website. This section will address these aspects.

Social Media

There are many social media platforms these days, (e.g. Pinterest, Instagram, LinkedIn and YouTube,) but perhaps the three that are most worthy of being concentrated on are Facebook, Twitter and Instagram which I have focused on below.

Facebook is great for networking and building community. It is the platform where people over forty seem to mostly congregate which often equates with my target readership.

It is great for creating events, advertising books and showcasing all our publishing successes, as well as being used to pose questions to other established writers.

If starting out as a writer on Facebook, 'befriend' as many other writers as you can and join some Facebook groups that interest you.

I love Facebook but try to keep my 'personal page' separate from the 'author page,' I have developed. An author page is necessary for advertising, which I would advise. I have found Facebook to be the most effective way of advertising my books.

Twitter is good for building your 'writing brand' and showcasing your authority, perhaps in an area you enjoy writing about – e.g. relationships or a particular place or era. You can 'follow' anyone, and anyone can 'follow' you.

The demographic is slightly younger in age than Facebook, probably thirty to fifty.

If starting out as a writer on Twitter, begin by following other writers as well as publishers, publications, agents, literary festivals and competitions that interest you.

I don't find Twitter effective for book sales, but it is good for networking and discovering what is going on in the world of publishing.

Instagram is a visual platform, comprising photographs which may or may not include captions. Users 'follow' one another and can like and comment on each other's posts. I don't use Instagram a great deal and opt to merely have a presence on there, where I share things such as cover reveals, deliveries of boxes of books, photographs of launch events or lovely places where I can sit and write.

If you are an author with a heavily illustrated book or your book contains some interesting settings which you can share photographs of, then you may be well-placed to spend some time on Instagram.

Social media can be extremely time consuming, in fact, sometimes I can log in and half an hour has disappeared before I know it, I call it *falling down a rabbit hole.*

You might need to limit yourself to a fixed time of day and a fixed amount of time per day, to scroll through your news feeds and respond to posts, otherwise it can soon eat into your valuable writing time. I try and limit my time to half an hour twice per day, but it rarely works out that way! I would also advise logging out of it completely whilst you are focussing on your writing.

Being part of online communities is effective for learning about submission opportunities, competitions and writing events. It's also a wonderful way for writers to support and promote each other.

The rule of thumb is eighty/twenty – that is eighty percent interacting with others, and sharing general information about writing, and twenty percent self-promotion of your own work or events you are involved with.

A prospective publisher would expect you to be on at least one social media channel and able to use it; for advertising your work and promoting events.

It is worth mentioning here that you don't have to use your *true* identity for your author brand and if you are writing under a pen name, you can use your book cover as your profile picture. Portray whatever you want and share as much, or as little, as you choose.

Having a Website

Your website is your 'shop window' onto the world and you should definitely have one. It should offer information about you, your successes, your news, publications, a blog and anything else you have to offer – for example, you might want to make yourself available to 'speak' in front of an audience, or to buddy up with another writer to swap extracts of writing to critique. Perhaps you will want to provide yourself with an extra income stream by offering yourself as an editor or proofreader.

Wordpress is a recommended website host here, as the support is good and the basic websites are free. You can also host your blog through your website.

Wordpress tends to be straightforward to set up, which is what you need when you're starting out. You might have the budget to pay someone to sort this out for you, but I can't reiterate the importance of ensuring you take control of your website once it is established.

You need to be able to update the pages regularly and you don't want to rely on someone else's timescale to do that. I have one friend whose website designer went into a new line of business entirely, leaving her without any way of being able to access the dashboard of her own website.

Blogging

Blogging and vlogging, (a video instead of written blog,) are excellent ways to showcase your writing and presentational abilities, and can be used to educate, inform or inspire others, whilst building a following of potential readers.

Some writers might blog on a particular occupation or relationship, perhaps linked to the type of novel they write. For example, a supernatural writer might blog about haunted places and someone writing a romantic novel might talk about how to find Mr/Mrs Right!

Using keywords or search terms throughout your blog (e.g. family dispute) can be a great way to bring people to your website and get them interested in something else you can offer, (like your novel!) I won't get into Search Engine Optimisation here as that is a whole new book – and not one I am equipped to write!

For the not-so-shy amongst you, a video blog (vlog) can be a powerful way of connecting with your readers, it's more personal than the written word and if you use YouTube as your medium, the mysterious algorithm will bring new readers to you.

There's a lot to think about here – far too much to do all at once. My best advice would be to start implementing the **thing** that mostly interests you about building your own writer platform. (e.g. setting up a Facebook author page or recording your first video.)

[cwb26.1] **Decide what your initial course of action will be to get your online presence up and running.**

Networking as a Writer

This next section extends on the last one. We have just discussed your *online* presence as a writer and we shall now turn to your *offline* one.

Online has the advantage of having a wider reach. All posts, videos and images are there forever, and will continue to bring new readers, and other writer contacts towards you.

Offline networking is also vital and will bring deeper and more personal connections, as well as really helping you to feel part of the new world you are inhabiting.

At this point in the first draft of your novel, you may be thinking about 'living as a writer' and wanting to immerse yourself as much as possible in the world of writing. That is wonderful!

Literature festivals offer amazing opportunities to network with other writers, to attend writing workshops and to listen to published writers who are a little further along the writing journey. They tend to be widely held in March and October. Because literature festivals are only annual events, open mic (spoken word) events can offer something more regular and can build your confidence in terms of putting your work and your writing self out there.

Advantages of attending open mic events:

- Being able to showcase your work and yourself as a writer.
- Becoming part of a community and network.
- Living as a writer and improving confidence.
- Listening and watching the styles of other writers and becoming more familiar with trends.
- Being less isolated as a writer.

Nerves can be a problem, however: below are a few tips on how to overcome them, (not involving wine!)

- Firstly, knowing that your work is the best it can be.
- Becoming familiar with the use of a microphone.
- Rehearsing your piece at home, possibly in front of a mirror and timing yourself. (Usually you will be given 3-5 minutes – long enough to read a short scene or a short chapter.) Take note of any occasions of stumbling over words.
- Going first can make you feel as though you are getting it out of the way, but by listening to several other writers before it is your turn, you give yourself time to focus outside yourself and get a feel for the theme and content.
- This time can also be used for regulating your breath.

Whilst reading:

- Ensure your position is comfortable and the right distance in relation to the microphone.

- Remember to breathe! Believe me, the first few times I did this, I literally ran out of breath!
- Read your work slowly and clearly, pausing where necessary to allow the words to sink in – overcome the temptation to rush. Here speaks the voice of experience!
- Imagine yourself as a 'vehicle' for your work – as though the words are emerging from behind you and are just travelling through you, to meet your audience. I know this sounds a bit 'out there' but doing this can offer some distance. Or you could pretend you are reading someone else's work.
- Look up from your page every so often – look out across your audience. Without eyeballing the same person – you will make them nervous!
- Hold a book or a folder containing your work – the 'shakes' will be less obvious. I still get these after years of reading in public.
- Ensure you read a piece where the audience will be in no doubt as to where it ends. There is nothing worse than a stunned silence where nobody realised that was actually *the end.* I simply say *thank you* at the end of a reading.
- Congratulate yourself afterwards – now you can have wine! Remember, it will not always be so nerve-wracking – all writers have to read for the first time somewhere! And as I am sure you are aware, writers are generally a friendly and supportive bunch.

Some other ways you can continue to 'live as a writer:'

- Subscribing to a writing magazine will keep you informed about opportunities and events, whilst being an excellent source for continued learning. (I recommend one called

Writing Magazine.)

- Attending writing courses – look out for workshops at literature festivals and writing days. You may want to aim even higher and consider an OU, BA or MA in Creative Writing or another accredited course. The Masters I did was one of the best investments I have ever made in myself as a writer. Not only did it increase my confidence in all areas of my writing career, it also opened many doors and offered a springboard from aspiring writer towards published and professional author. And I must mention here that I offer both face-to-face and online courses. Visit www.mariafrankland.co.uk for more information.
- Forming or joining a writing group – writing can be a lonely and solitary activity, therefore joining an established writing group can be an excellent way to stay connected to other writers. It also offers the opportunity to help one another and provide feedback to one another. If there isn't one in your area, consider starting one up of your own.
- Finding a writing buddy. This can keep you motivated and accountable and offers an excellent opportunity for you to swap and comment on each other's writing.

I hope that at this point in the book, you are feeling truly excited about your future as a writer. Keep going, keep moving forward, keep writing. The end of that first draft of your novel gets closer with every word you write.

Perhaps you can give some thought to what your cover might look like, what the blurb on the back of your book might say, where you will have your book launch. Your hard work will soon start to pay off!

Your Cover Letter to Agents and Publishers

There are two principal routes to being published. The first, and the one the majority of novelists initially seek, is the traditional way, whereby a contract is secured with a publishing company, and/or a literary agent.

The second is independent publishing, whereby you have full autonomy over your work, and publish it yourself – cutting out the middle man, and getting it straight in front of your readers.

There are, as with anything, pros and cons for each, and I will discuss both throughout the remainder of this book.

If you choose to go down the traditional route, part of the submission package you will assemble to sell your manuscripts to an agent or publisher, will be your cover letter.

This will be the first thing a prospective agent or publisher looks at and should therefore be flawless. The synopsis, (which I will cover in the next section) and your first three chapters, (which need to be thoroughly edited,) complete the make up of this 'package.'

In your letter, the following information must be included: your name and address, any website details, your email address and home and mobile phone numbers.

If possible, address the recipient by name, use titles, not first names. Double check the publisher's or agent's website to ensure accuracy. *You don't want to give them any reason to reject your submission!*

[cwb28.1] **The notes you make for the following prompts** can be adapted according to the requirements of individual publishers, and will provide you with a basis from which to write your covering letter.

Try to respond to each point, if you can!

1. A summary of your novel in two lines (your 'pitch,' useful to have in mind for when anyone asks you what your novel is 'about.') *By now you've probably started telling people that you are writing a novel and when they ask 'what's it about?' you need a concise and intriguing response!*
2. Why you've written your novel (What has inspired you? What your interest is, what your knowledge or experience in the subject matter is.) *Just a couple of lines will do here.*
3. Who it might be of interest to (your intended readership – you could mention here whether you already have a potential list of readers built up through Facebook friends or followers of a blog.) *In this day and age, the marketing publishers will do, is very limited. This shows your willingness to market yourself.*
4. What novels you like to read and what has influenced

you. (You could compare your novel here to that of other writers. Where will your novel sit in the market?) *It is also important here to know exactly which genre you are writing in. Many publishing houses have specific people handling specific genres. In which section of the bookshop, will your novel sit?*

5. Previous publications and successes in your writing, (no matter how seemingly small, competition wins, seconds or runners up, inclusions in anthologies, etc.) *This offers social proof of your talent and also demonstrates an investment in yourself as a writer.*
6. Events and courses you attend or have attended. *More social proof, more investment in yourself and this also shows the commitment you have to improving your craft.*
7. What you would be willing/able to do to help to promote your novel. *When you're a 'new shiny thing,' your publisher will do some marketing. But within a short space of time, even a month, they will move onto the next 'new shiny thing.'*
8. Any other relevant biographical information, (try to showcase something of your personality here. Show them you are a writer with whom they can build a positive working rapport.) *This would also be a good place to say why you have chosen them to be your publisher.*

[cwb28.2] **Now that you have some notes, you might like to use the following framework to draft your letter.**

Opening Paragraph

- The title of your novel and it's genre. At this stage you need to show the publisher or agent what type of book you have written so they can decide whether it will fit into their current list.

- A line or two which captures the essence of the book. This should be a concise and targeted summary.

Paragraph Two

- The book's approximate word count.
- A confirmation of completion, or an expected date.
- A comparable title or two to enable them to know whether your book is a saleable product.
- What is its 'Unique Selling Point?' What will interest readers about it?

Paragraph Three

- Talk about you as a writer – market yourself! Try to offer a hint of your personality through your writing.
- Include a brief biography in relation to your writing career.
- Include any publishing or competition successes.

Paragraph Four

- Add information about your web presence.
- Acknowledge how you will be involved in the marketing of your book.
- Include any unique media contacts you may possess.

You will need to adapt this to the needs and requirements of each publisher or literary agent. (More about their roles soon.)

Writing a Synopsis

Part of the submission package you will assemble to 'sell' your proposed novel to an agent or publisher is called a synopsis.

This is an overview of your book but differs from the 'blurb' which goes on your book jacket – a blurb is designed to attract readers, rather than publishers and agents.

If you haven't already, you might want to try drafting your blurb as it is a great way to really nail down your story to the key characters and events. A good way to start your blurb is with your pitch, (mentioned in the previous section,) and ending with a question. You could look at some already published books for examples.

The synopsis is a more comprehensive and detailed account which showcases your ability to write and is purposeful in that it will present the gist of the plot, the characters and their motives and very importantly, the ending.

A word of warning! They are harder to write than they first appear and normally need several revisions. Writers in my face to face courses report them as being extremely beneficial, especially if written whilst the novel is still progressing. As with the blurb, thought given to your synopsis at this stage can help with the focus and direction of the novel.

When you get to the point of submission, your synopsis will need adapting, along with your cover letter, for each publisher or agent, depending on their requirements.

A synopsis should:

1. Offer a clear idea of what sort of book you are offering.
2. Suggest what its market might be.
3. Be around 750 words, (this is really hard!!)
4. Be typed in 12pt on single-sided A4 paper.
5. Be single spaced with numbered pages.
6. Include your name and the novel's title on each page in the header.
7. Include the genre and approximate word count on the first page.
8. Use the first sentence as a hook.
9. Give a broad outline summary of the whole story, recounting the central storyline, (not a chapter by chapter summary.)
10. Name and introduce the main characters, (in capitals at their first mention.)
11. Start with the main character and whatever they are facing.
12. Describe the novel's location and era.
13. Mention any major scenes or crises.
14. Include a brief reference to any significant sub-plots.
15. Be written in story form rather than factual.

16. Include character emotion and motivation.
17. Be in present tense.
18. Be in third person.
19. Be clear and straightforward.
20. Be consistent in tone with the novel.
21. Be accurate and without typos, poor spelling or grammatical errors.
22. Be as well-written as the novel itself.

Phew! That's quite a list. Good luck!

[cwb29.1] **Do a first draft of your synopsis,** adhering to the above 'checklist.

Whatever stage you're at in your novel, you will find that this process enhances your novel's path forward.

Getting Published

Here's the big one! The finale! This is what most writers working on a novel are aiming for.

Each novelist has their own definition of success. For some, it might be for family and friends to enjoy their novel. For others, it might be having their book stocked in a local bookshop, whilst some writers may aspire to the production of their novel for the mass-market.

Whatever your level of ambition, it can be a good idea to write shorter items, such as short stories, flash fiction and poetry for submission.

These are great for building up a 'CV' of writing successes which will do wonders for your confidence as a writer and make you an attractive proposition for prospective publishers – remember that cover letter!

There is no feeling like seeing your work in print. Taking delivery of that box of books and holding your book in your hands. Here are some ideas to make this a reality:

Writing Magazine

Subscribing to a writing magazine can offer a wealth of competitions, including lots of debuts novel competitions. Often within these magazines, details can be found about publishers and agents that are seeking particular types of submission, particularly with smaller or newer publishing houses. I should be on a commission for *Writing Magazine,* the amount of times I have recommended it!

Competitions

Debut novel competitions, many of them are offered for free, worldwide, throughout the year. There are plenty of websites around that collate details of upcoming competition opportunities. There are well-known novel competitions, such as *The Richard and Judy Bookclub, the Daily Mail First Novel Competition* and the *Good Housekeeping First Novel Competition.*

This is how I got started with my first novel. It made the shortlist of an international competition which was the boost I needed to keep going. I am absolute proof that these competitions are well worth entering.

Literary Agents

A literary agent is paid to represent you, (usually at a fee of 15% of any royalties) and also to negotiate the best deal on your behalf. Each agent usually has their own website. They act as an 'intermediary' between you and the publisher, and these days can be as difficult to secure, as a publisher.

Some writers wonder whether or not they should recruit an agent. I would say that getting in with a 'bigger' publisher is impossible without an agent but it's worth seeing what they will offer you in return for their 15%. All too often, writers jump at an offer like it's the Holy Grail so make sure they are offering you *as much* as you are offering them - i.e. your precious book.

Publishers

Many publishers will not take a new author directly but will prefer the introduction to be made through an agent. Some independent publishers might be more inclined to accept an unsolicited approach.

They will generally assist you with editing, cover design, formatting and book production, as well as launching your book and marketing but in return, they will usually take at least 20% of your royalties, which is a lot, especially when combined with the 40% a bookshop will take. After the printer has taken their cut too, there's precious little left for you, the author.

Publishers will, (but not always, these days,) sweeten this pill by offering you an advance. Again, as with your agent, choose carefully. Make sure your publisher is going to work for you.

And never, ever, ever, ever, ever part with any money. I've had several of my novelists, and two poets, contact me in a flurry of excitement saying they've been snapped up by a publisher.

When I've taken a closer look, it's been a 'vanity' publisher, masquerading as a genuine publishing house and requesting initial fees in the region of two thousand pounds. Get in touch with me if you're not sure!

Magazines and Newspapers

There are many opportunities to get short stories into magazines, particularly in women's magazines, and often they pay quite well. It is an excellent way to build your list of successes as previously mentioned. Some offer annual novel competitions.

Independent Publishing

You could bypass the gatekeepers, (agents, competitions and publishers,) and get your work straight in front of your readers, and keep all the profit. You can produce your work as a paperback, e-book and audio book. The following points need to be kept in mind:

1. Your writing must be polished and edited (preferably professionally.)
2. Consider having the book cover professionally designed.
3. You will need to research the formatting process.
4. You will need to be prepared to have a budget for advertising to get your work in front of readers.
5. You might want to order a box of author copies to sell directly to your family and friends, and at any launch events and promotions you organise.

There is a lot of work and learning involved in doing this, and if you are interested, I would recommend Mark Dawson and Joanna Penn as the masters of independent publishing!

Again, I should be on a commission for the amount of times I recommend their wisdom to other writers.

Personally, I have been traditionally published and have published independently, (setting up Autonomy Press – my own small publishing company, though it is not necessary to actually set up a company, you can do it under your own name.

The secret is to make your novel **indistinguishable** from any mass produced novel, and have a marketing budget. Facebook ads and Amazon ads work well for me but initially, there's a lot of learning and trial and error involved.

I totally understand why authors yearn for the kudos and expertise of a traditional publisher but for me, independence is something I love and I would definitely recommend it, if you are prepared to put the hours in!

Whichever way you go, I wish you all the luck in the world as you near completion of your first draft of your novel. Keep on enjoying the journey and keep me posted. I will be first in the queue for my signed copy – glass of bubbly in hand!

Before you go...

Join my 'keep in touch' list to receive a free book, and to be kept posted of other freebies, special offers and new releases. Being in touch with other writers is one of the best things about being an author and creative writing teacher. You can visit www.mariafrankland.co.uk to join and receive a free copy of The 7 S.E.C.R.E.T.S. to Achieving your Writing Dreams.

I'd love to know what you thought of Write a Novel in a Year, and always welcome feedback, both positive and not-so-positive! The easiest way to do this is by leaving a review, and you can leave one by revisiting the Amazon product page.

It's great to know what you want more of, or not, as the case may be! It only needs to be a line or three, but also helps other writers find the book.

Thank you!

This book is derived from a year-long online course which includes video, access to an online support group, further writing tasks and examples, links to further reading and the option of one-to-one support.

See https://mariafrankland.co.uk/how-to-write-a-novel/ for more information.

By the Same Author

How-to Books for Writers

Write your Life Story in a Year
Write a Collection of Poetry in a Year
Write a Collection of Short Stories in a Year

Memoir

Don't Call me Mum! A mother's story about being pushed to the brink

Psychological Thrillers

Left Hanging: What price would you pay to save your marriage?
The Man Behind Closed Doors: The other side of domestic bliss
The Yorkshire Dipper: What would you risk to bring the truth to the surface?
The Last Cuckoo: When ghosts live on in stepfamilies
Hit and Run: He was dead before she really knew him
The Hen Party: First there were ten. Then there were nine

Poetry

Poetry for the Newly Married 40 Something: How to get from

BY THE SAME AUTHOR

Tinder to altar

Acknowledgements

I'd like to say a huge thank you to my husband, Michael, for his support and expertise in the latter stages of this book.

Thanks also to all the writers who have taken this course over the years, either in the classroom or by distance learning. Your feedback has enabled me to tweak and refine the course, and many of you have become friends too!

Thank you to Prince Henry's Grammar School in Otley for the space and platform to offer my creative writing courses, and I also want to acknowledge Leeds Trinity University where I completed my teaching and English degree, and then my Masters in Creative Writing.

These degrees took me to a new level as a writer and enabled me to pass on my own learning through the courses I've written and now offer.

And lastly, can I thank you, the 'student' of this book, for choosing to share your writing journey with me, and for allowing me to share what I know to help you write your own novel. It is a true honour and I hope you will keep me posted of your success!

About the Author

Maria Frankland's life began at 40 when she began making a living from her own writing and becoming a teacher of creative writing. The springboard into making writing her whole career was made possible by the MA in Creative Writing she undertook at Leeds Trinity University.

The rich tapestry of life with all its turbulent times has enabled her to pour experience, angst and lessons learned into the writing of her novels and poetry. She recognises that the darkest places can exist within family relationships and this is reflected in the domestic thrillers she writes. She strongly advocates the wonderful power and therapeutic properties of writing.

She is a 'born 'n' bred' Yorkshirewoman, a mother of two, and has recently found her own 'happy ever after' after marrying again. Still in her forties, she is now going to dedicate the rest of her working life to writing her own books, whilst inspiring and motivating other writers to achieve their own writing dreams.

You can connect with me on:

- https://www.mariafrankland.co.uk
- https://twitter.com/writermaria_f
- https://www.facebook.com/writermariafrank
- https://www.autonomypress.co.uk

Subscribe to my newsletter:

✉ https://mailchi.mp/f69ecf568e7b/writersignup

Printed in Great Britain
by Amazon